# Illusion of Online Safety

## Digital Defense Manual for Young Minds

HAFIZ AFZAAL

ISBN: 9798301149474
Imprint: Independently published

# DEDICATION

Hey there, digital explorers!

This book is dedicated to all young people navigating the vast digital universe. Whether you're just starting your online journey or you're already a seasoned internet user, this guide is for you. You deserve to explore, create, connect, and thrive in the digital world safely and confidently.

Special dedication goes to all the kids who have ever felt unsure, scared, or overwhelmed by online challenges. Your safety matters, your privacy matters, and your digital well-being matters. This book is also dedicated to the young digital citizens who stand up against cyberbullying, support others online, and help make the internet a better place for everyone.

Let's work together to create a safer, kinder, and more awesome digital world!

# ACKNOWLEDGEMENTS

Creating a comprehensive guide to digital safety takes a village, and I am deeply grateful to everyone who contributed to making this book possible.

First and foremost, I want to thank the countless young people who shared their experiences, challenges, and triumphs in navigating the digital world. Your stories have helped shape this book into a practical and relatable guide for others.

Special thanks to the cybersecurity experts, educators, parents, and digital safety advocates who provided valuable insights and reviewed the content to ensure its accuracy and relevance. Your expertise has been invaluable in creating a resource that truly serves young readers.

To my family, thank you for understanding the importance of this project and supporting me through the writing process. Your encouragement and patience made this book possible.

To my readers, thank you for taking this important step in becoming safer and smarter digital citizens. Your commitment to learning about digital safety will help create a better online world for everyone.

# CONTENTS

PREFACE .................................................................................... xi

**Welcome to the Digital Universe** ........................................ 1

What is Cyberspace? .......................................................... 2

Your Digital Identity ........................................................... 3

The Good, the Bad, and the Risky ...................................... 4

Digital Footprints: Everything Leaves a Trace ..................... 6

Conclusion .......................................................................... 7

Coming Up Next ................................................................. 7

*Your Thought on Digital Universe Safety* ......................... 9

**The Illusion of Online Safety** ............................................ 10

Why We Feel Safe Online .................................................... 11

Common Misconceptions ..................................................... 12

Real Stories from Young People ......................................... 13

Understanding Digital Risks ............................................... 15

The Importance of Digital Street Smarts ............................ 16

Conclusion .......................................................................... 17

Coming Up Next ................................................................. 17

*Your Thought on Online Safety Illusion* .......................... 18

**Your Personal Information is Precious** ............................... 19

What is Personal Information? ............................................ 20

Why Do People Want Your Data? ....................................... 21

The Data Collection Game .................................................. 22

Privacy vs. Convenience ..................................................... 24

Your Rights in the Digital World ........................................ 25

Conclusion .......................................................................... 26

Coming Up Next ................................................................. 26

*Your Thought on Personal Information Safety* ..................................... 28

## Cyber Threats ....................................................................... 29

Understanding Different Types of Cyber Threats ..................... 30

Identifying Cyber Threats ............................................................ 33

Virus and Malware Warning Signs .......................................... 34

Phishing and Scam Red Flags: ................................................... 36

Identity Theft Warning Signs: ................................................... 38

Experiencing Cyberbullying and Harassment: ....................... 40

Conclusion ...................................................................................... 41

Coming Up Next ........................................................................... 42

*Your Understanding about Cyber Threats* .................................. 43

## Social Media Safety ......................................................... 44

Platform-Specific Safety Tips ..................................................... 45

Privacy Settings Made Simple ................................................... 49

Think Before You Post ................................................................. 51

Dealing with Unwanted Attention ............................................ 53

Photo and Video Sharing Safety ................................................ 54

Conclusion ...................................................................................... 54

Coming Up Next ........................................................................... 55

*Your Thought on Social Media Safety* ........................................ 56

## Gaming World Safety ....................................................... 57

Online Gaming Risks .................................................................... 58

Understanding the Real Cost ...................................................... 59

Chat Safety While Gaming .......................................................... 61

Protecting Your Gaming Accounts ............................................ 62

Dealing with Toxic Players .......................................................... 63

Conclusion ...................................................................................... 64

Coming Up Next..................................................................65

*Your Perception about Gaming World safety*....................66

**Password Power** ............................................................67

Creating Super-Strong Passwords ..........................68

Password Manager Basics ......................................69

Setting Up Your Digital Vault................................70

Two-Factor Authentication Made Easy .................71

Biometric Security .................................................72

Password DO's and DON'Ts .................................73

Conclusion .............................................................74

Coming Up Next.....................................................74

*Your Believe About Password Strength*....................75

**Device Defense** ............................................................76

Protecting Your Smartphone .................................77

App Permission Management.................................79

Updates and Security Patches ...............................80

Using Public Wi-Fi Safely .....................................81

VPN Basics for Young Users .................................82

Conclusion .............................................................83

Coming Up Next.....................................................83

*Your Experience With Your Device Defense* .................84

**Safe Browsing Habits**..................................................85

Browser Security Settings ......................................86

Safe Search Techniques .........................................87

Download Safety .....................................................88

Ad Blockers and Security Extensions.....................89

Recognizing Fake Websites ....................................90

Conclusion ......................................................................... 91

Coming Up Next ................................................................ 92

*Your Thought on Safe Browsing Habits* ................................ 93

## Digital Communication Safety ................................... 94

Email Security ..................................................................... 95

Messaging App Safety ........................................................ 97

Video Chat Safety ............................................................... 98

Dealing with Unknown Contacts ........................................ 99

Sharing Files Safely .......................................................... 100

Conclusion ....................................................................... 101

Coming Up Next .............................................................. 101

*Your Thought on Digital Communication Safety* ............... 102

## Being a Digital Detective ........................................ 103

Fact-Checking Skills ......................................................... 104

Understanding Digital Manipulation ................................ 106

Safe Research Techniques ................................................. 108

Conclusion ....................................................................... 110

Coming Up Next .............................................................. 110

*Your Strategy Being a Digital Detective* ........................... 111

## Becoming a Digital Citizen ...................................... 112

Digital Ethics and Responsibility ..................................... 113

Reporting Problems .......................................................... 116

Conclusion ....................................................................... 118

Coming Up Next .............................................................. 118

*Your Understanding of a Good Digital Citizen* .................. 119

## When Things Go Wrong .......................................... 120

Signs You've Been Hacked ................................................ 121

What to Do If You're Being Cyberbullied ........................... 122

Dealing with Online Harassment ................................... 123

How to Report ................................................... 124

Recovery Steps After an Incident ................................. 125

Conclusion ...................................................... 126

Coming Up Next .................................................. 127

*Your Thought on Cyber Crisis Strategy* .......................... 128

**Creating Your Safety Plan** .................................... 129

Personal Security Checklist ...................................... 130

Family Discussion Guide .......................................... 131

Regular Security Audit Guide ..................................... 132

Digital Safety Agreement Template ................................ 133

Conclusion ...................................................... 135

*Your Thought on Cyber Safety Plan* .............................. 137

**Glossary of Terms** ............................................ 138

Scenario 1: The Strange Friend Request ........................... 140

Scenario 2: The Game Trade Offer ................................. 140

Scenario 3: The Viral Challenge .................................. 141

**Digital Safety Pledges** ....................................... 142

Personal Digital Safety Pledge ................................... 142

Family Online Safety Agreement ................................... 143

Digital Citizenship Commitment ................................... 144

Challenge 1: 7-Day Digital Security Sprint ....................... 145

Challenge 2: Digital Detective Training .......................... 145

Challenge 3: Online Safety Ambassador ............................ 145

**Digital Security Master Checklists** ........................... 147

Daily Security Checklist ......................................... 147

Weekly Security Checklist ................................................................ 147

Monthly Security Audit .................................................................. 148

Social Media Safety Checklist ......................................................... 148

Device Security Checklist ............................................................... 149

Gaming Account Security ............................................................... 150

Emergency Response Checklist ....................................................... 150

Family Safety Checklist .................................................................. 151

New Device Setup Checklist ........................................................... 152

Digital Footprint Cleanup Checklist ............................................... 152

Safe Browsing Checklist ................................................................. 153

Understanding Your Child's Digital World ...................................... 155

Conversation Starters ..................................................................... 156

Family Tech Rules Template ........................................................... 156

**Family Safety Agreement Template** .................................................. 157

**Glossary of Terms** ......................................................................... 158

Further Reading ............................................................................. 159

# PREFACE

Dear Digital Explorer,

Imagine you're about to embark on an incredible journey through a vast digital universe. This universe is filled with amazing opportunities, exciting adventures, and endless possibilities. You can connect with friends across the globe, learn anything at the click of a button, create and share your own content, and explore virtual worlds that spark your imagination.

But here's something interesting to think about: Would you walk into a busy city blindfolded? Would you leave your house with all the doors unlocked? Would you share your diary with complete strangers? Probably not! Yet every day, many young people do the digital equivalent of these things without even realizing it.

I wrote this book because I've seen too many young people get hurt online simply because no one taught them how to protect themselves in the digital world. As a cybersecurity expert who has spent years investigating digital crimes and helping people recover from cyber attacks, I've witnessed firsthand how a single click, an innocent post, or a moment of trust can sometimes lead to serious consequences.

But don't worry – this isn't a book full of scary stories meant to frighten you away from the internet. Instead, think of it as your personal guide to becoming a digital superhero! Just as superheroes need to understand both their powers and their vulnerabilities, you need to know how to use your digital powers wisely while protecting yourself from cyber villains.

This book is different from other online safety guides. We won't just tell you what not to do – we'll show you how to do things better. Through real stories, interactive exercises, and practical tips, you'll learn how to:

- Spot digital dangers before they can harm you
- Protect your personal information like a pro
- Create an awesome (and safe) online presence
- Help others stay safe in the digital world
- Handle problems if things go wrong

- Become a responsible digital citizen

Throughout this book, you'll find:

- ✓ Eye-opening "Did You Know?" facts that might surprise you
- ✓ Fun quizzes to test your knowledge
- ✓ Real-life stories from young people like you
- ✓ Cool activities to practice your new skills
- ✓ Checklists to keep you on track

The digital world is constantly changing, and that's why this book teaches you how to think critically and make smart decisions, rather than just following a set of rules that might be outdated tomorrow. Consider this book your training ground for developing "digital street smarts" – skills that will serve you well throughout your life.

Remember, being safe online doesn't mean being scared or missing out on fun. It means being smart, aware, and prepared. Think of it like learning to swim – once you know how to do it safely, you can have a great time in the water without worrying about drowning.

As you read this book, imagine we're having a conversation. Feel free to take notes, highlight important parts, and most importantly, put what you learn into practice. Share your knowledge with friends and family – because when it comes to online safety, we're all in this together.

Are you ready to become a digital safety expert? Turn the page, and let's begin your journey to becoming a smart, safe, and savvy digital citizen!


Stay safe and have fun,

Hafiz Afzaal


P.S. To parents, teachers, and guardians reading this: You'll find special sections throughout the book designed to help you support young people in their digital safety journey. Remember, the best way to keep kids safe online is to keep the lines of communication open and stay involved in their digital lives.

# CHAPTER 1

## Welcome to the Digital Universe

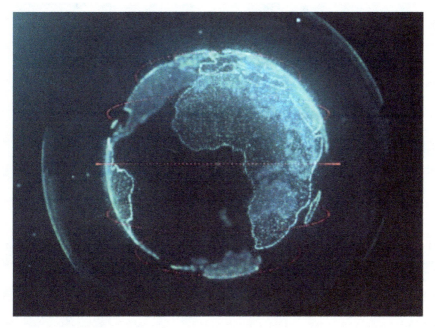

Photo: Adobe Photo Stock

Hey there, digital explorer! If you're reading this, you're probably already familiar with using smartphones, tablets, computers, and the internet. Maybe you use these devices to chat with friends, play games, watch videos, or do homework. But have you ever stopped to think about what this amazing digital universe really is, and how you can navigate it safely? Let's embark on an exciting journey to understand digital world better!

## What is Cyberspace?

Photo: Adobe Photo Stock

Imagine you're standing in the middle of an invisible city - one that exists all around us but can't be seen or touched. This invisible city is called cyberspace, and it's where all our digital activities happen. Every time you send a text message, that message travels through this invisible city to reach your friend. When you watch a YouTube video, you're visiting a special building in this city where videos are stored. When you play an online game, you're entering a digital playground where people from all over the world can meet and play together.

Think of cyberspace as a massive network of invisible highways connecting millions of digital devices. These highways carry all sorts of information - pictures, messages, videos, games, and more - at lightning speed. Just like a real city has different neighborhoods (some safe, some not so safe), cyberspace also has different areas that we need to learn about to stay safe.

But here's something really cool about cyberspace: it's always growing and changing! Every day, new websites are created, new apps are launched, and new ways of connecting with others are developed. It's like a city that never stops building new roads, houses, and places to explore.

However, just as you wouldn't walk into a strange neighborhood without knowing anything about it, you shouldn't explore cyberspace without understanding how it works. That's where digital street smarts come in - the knowledge and skills you need to stay safe while enjoying all the amazing things cyberspace has to offer.

## Your Digital Identity

Photo: Adobe Photo Stock

Have you ever thought about who you are in the digital world? Your digital identity is like your online self - it's made up of all the information about you that exists in cyberspace. Think of it as your digital twin who represents you whenever you're online.

Your digital identity includes obvious things like your social media profiles, email accounts, and gaming usernames. But it also includes things you might not think about, like:

- The websites you visit
- The videos you watch

- The games you play
- The things you like and share
- The comments you make
- The photos you post
- Your online search history

What makes your digital identity special is that it can be different from your real-life identity in some ways. Online, you might be known as "SportsFan123" or "ArtisticDragon," and that's okay! But remember, even when you're using a different name or avatar, your actions online are still connected to the real you.

Your digital identity is like a puzzle that gets bigger every time you do something online. Each post, like, comment, or share adds another piece to this puzzle. That's why it's super important to think carefully about what pieces you want to add. Ask yourself: "Is this something I want to be part of my digital identity?"

Here's something really important to remember: your digital identity isn't just about who you say you are - it's also about what others can learn about you online. Sometimes, people can piece together information about you from different places in cyberspace, like putting together pieces of a jigsaw puzzle. That's why we need to be careful about what information we share online.

## The Good, the Bad, and the Risky

The digital universe is a lot like a huge amusement park. It's filled with exciting opportunities and fun experiences, but it also has some rides that might be dangerous if you're not careful. Let's explore what makes cyberspace both awesome and risky.

### The Good:

Cyberspace has transformed our world in amazing ways. You can video chat with a friend who lives on the other side of the planet, learn any skill through online tutorials, or explore virtual museums from your bedroom. You can find communities of people who share your interests, whether you're into coding, crafting, or collecting rocks. The internet has made learning more accessible and fun than ever before!

For example, during the recent global pandemic, cyberspace became our classroom, our playground, and our meeting place. Students could continue their education, families could stay connected, and friends could still hang out - all thanks to the digital universe.

## The Bad:

Unfortunately, just like in the real world, there are people in cyberspace who don't have good intentions. Some create viruses that can harm your devices, while others try to trick people into sharing private information. There are also cyberbullies who use the internet to hurt others' feelings or spread mean rumors.

## The Risky:

Then there are things that aren't necessarily bad but can be risky if you're not careful. For instance, playing online games can be super fun, but some games might try to get you to spend real money on virtual items. Social media can help you stay connected with friends, but oversharing personal information could put your privacy at risk.

**Real World Example:** Sarah, a 12-year-old gamer, loved playing an online game where she could create her own virtual world. She made many friends in the game, and one day, someone she met offered to give her rare in-game items for free. All they needed was her account password. Luckily, Sarah remembered that sharing passwords is never safe, no matter how friendly someone seems, and declined the offer.

## Digital Footprints: Everything Leaves a Trace

Photo: Adobe Photo Stock

Imagine walking on a beach - every step you take leaves a footprint in the sand. In cyberspace, everything you do leaves a digital footprint, but unlike beach footprints, these don't wash away with the tide. Your digital footprints can last for a very long time, sometimes forever!

### Active Footprints:

Your digital footprints encompass both active and passive traces of your online activities. Active footprints refer to the intentional actions you take, such as posting on social media, participating in online forums, leaving comments on blogs or videos, writing reviews, and message you send. These actions are deliberate, and you are aware that you are creating a record of your presence.

### Passive Footprints:

On the other hand, passive footprints are generated without your direct awareness. These include data that is collected simply by your online behavior, such as the websites you visit, the searches you conduct, and the metadata associated with your internet usage. Even if you don't consciously put information out there, your digital actions leave behind significant traces that can reveal a lot about your habits, preferences, and even your identity. Understanding both types of footprints is crucial for managing your online privacy and security effectively.

Think of your digital footprints like dropping tiny breadcrumbs everywhere you go online. Each crumb might seem small and unimportant, but together they can tell quite a story about who you are, what you like, and what you do.

**Real World Example:** Max, a 14-year-old student, wanted to join his school's leadership team. When the teachers were reviewing applications, they looked up the candidates online (yes, adults do this!). They found that Max had left mean comments on several YouTube videos months ago. Even though Max had grown and changed since then, those digital footprints affected how people saw him.

The good news is that you have control over many of your digital footprints! By thinking before you post, being kind online, and understanding privacy settings, you can create positive digital footprints that you'll be proud of later.

## Conclusion

Welcome to the beginning of your journey to becoming a savvy digital citizen! In this chapter, we've learned that cyberspace is an incredible place full of opportunities, but it requires understanding and careful navigation. Your digital identity is precious and worth protecting, and your digital footprints can have lasting impacts on your life.

Remember, being online isn't about being perfect - it's about being smart, safe, and responsible. As you continue reading this book, you'll learn more specific strategies and tools to help you make the most of your digital adventures while staying safe.

## Coming Up Next

Get ready to dive deeper into the fascinating world of online safety in our next chapter, "The Illusion of Online Safety." We'll explore why people sometimes feel safer online than they should, and we'll share real stories from young people just like you who learned important lessons about digital security. You'll discover the difference between feeling safe and being safe online, and learn some cool tricks to spot potential risks before they become problems. So, keep reading - your journey to becoming a digital safety expert is just beginning!

# Your Thought on Digital Universe Safety

1. What parts of your digital identity do you share online without thinking about it? Are there things you should be more careful about sharing?

2. How would you explain "digital footprints" to a younger sibling? Why do they matter?

3. Think about your favorite online activities. What are the good and risky aspects of each one?

# Did you know?

Every day, humans create 2.5 quintillion bytes of data - that's equivalent to 250,000 times the printed material in the U.S. Library of Congress. By the time you finish reading this sentence, over 500 hours of video will have been uploaded to YouTube!

# CHAPTER 2

## The Illusion of Online Safety

Photo: Adobe Photo Stock

Have you ever felt super safe and cozy while browsing the internet in your room? Maybe you're wrapped up in your favorite blanket, lying on your bed, scrolling through social media or playing your favorite game. Everything feels secure because you're in your own space, right? Well, that's what we call the **"illusion" of online safety** - when we feel safe but might not actually be as safe as we think. Let's explore why this happens and how we can protect ourselves better!

## Why We Feel Safe Online

Photo: Adobe Photo Stock

When we're online, several things trick our brains into feeling safer than we actually are. First, there's the "bedroom effect" - we're physically in a safe place, so our brain assumes we're completely safe. Think about it: you're in your room, maybe with your door closed, possibly with your family just down the hall. How could anything bad happen here?

Then there's the "screen barrier" - because we're interacting through a screen, our brain doesn't process potential dangers the same way it would in the real world. It's like watching a scary movie - part of your brain knows it's not real because it's happening on a screen. But unlike a movie, the internet connects us to real people and real situations.

Another reason we feel safe is the "control illusion" - we think we're in control because we can choose what to click on, which friend requests to accept, and what information to share. But here's the thing: just because we control what we share doesn't mean we control what happens to that information once it's out there.

Sometimes we feel safe simply because nothing bad has happened yet. It's like thinking you don't need to wear a bike helmet because you've never fallen off your bike before. But smart cyclists know that wearing a helmet isn't about what happened yesterday - it's about being prepared for what might happen tomorrow.

## Common Misconceptions

Photo: Adobe Photo Stock

Let's bust some common myths about online safety that many young people (and even adults!) believe:

### Private accounts are completely private

Even with a private account, your information isn't completely secure. People can take screenshots, share your posts, or hack into accounts. Plus, the social media platforms themselves still have access to everything you post. Think of it like having a diary with a lock - while the lock keeps most people out, someone who really wants to could still find a way to open it.

## I'm too young for hackers to target me

Actually, young people are often targeted specifically because they might be less careful with their information. Your accounts, devices, and personal information are valuable to cybercriminals regardless of your age. They might use your account to scam others, steal your parents' credit card information, or collect data about your family.

## I only friend/follow people I know

This seems safe, but do you really know everyone you're connected with online? Sometimes people create fake accounts pretending to be kids your age. They might copy profile pictures from real kids and even pretend to know people from your school. It's like someone wearing a really good costume - from far away, they might look like someone you know.

## My passwords are strong enough

Many people think adding a number such as "1" or a special character such as "!" at the end makes it a strong password. But modern password-cracking tools can figure these out pretty quickly. It's like having a bike lock that looks tough but can be opened with a paperclip - it gives you a false sense of security.

## Bad things only happen to people who aren't careful

This is a dangerous myth. Even very careful people can become victims of cybercrime. Sometimes new types of scams or hacks emerge that no one has seen before. That's why it's important to stay informed and keep learning about online safety.

## Real Stories from Young People

Let's look at some real experiences from kids just like you. (Names have been changed for privacy.)

## Jamie's Story: The Friend Request

Jamie, age 13, received a friend request from someone claiming to be a new student at their school. The profile looked real - it had photos, posts, and even mutual friends. Jamie accepted the request and started chatting with them. The "new student" started asking personal questions and eventually tried to convince Jamie to meet in person. Fortunately, Jamie told their parents, who discovered it was a fake account created by someone pretending to be a teenager.

## Maya's Story: The "Free" Game Offer

Maya, age 11, downloaded a "free" game that her friends were playing. The game itself was free, but it kept pushing her to buy special items and power-ups. Before she realized it, she had spent $200 using her parents' linked credit card. She learned that "free" games often use tricks to get you to spend real money.

## Alex's Story: The Shared Photo

Alex, age 14, sent a silly but embarrassing photo to their best friend through a messaging app that claimed photos would disappear after viewing. The friend took a screenshot and shared it with others as a joke. The photo spread through their school, causing Alex significant distress. They learned that nothing truly disappears once it's sent online.

## Sarah's Story: The Password Problem

Sarah, age 12, used the same password for all her accounts because it was easier to remember. When one gaming site she used was hacked, the attackers gained access to all her other accounts, including her email and social media. She had to spend weeks recovering her accounts and creating new, unique passwords.

## Understanding Digital Risks

Photo: Adobe Photo Stock

Digital risks come in many forms, and understanding them is the first step to protecting yourself. Think of them like different types of weather you need to prepare for:

### Cyberbullying:
Like a thunderstorm that can strike unexpectedly, cyberbullying can happen to anyone. It might come from people you know or strangers online. The anonymity of the internet sometimes makes people act in ways they never would face-to-face.

### Identity Theft:
Similar to someone stealing your backpack, digital identity theft is when someone takes your personal information to pretend to be you or to gain access to your accounts. This can happen through hacking, phishing (trying to trick you into giving away information), or collecting small pieces of information you share across different platforms.

### Online Scams:
These are like mirages in a desert - things that look real but aren't. Online

scams might offer amazing prizes, free games, or exclusive items to trick you into clicking dangerous links or sharing personal information.

### Privacy Breaches:

Even when you think your information is private, it might not be. Apps and websites collect data about you, and this information can be leaked or stolen. It's like whispering a secret that ends up being heard by more people than you intended.

## The Importance of Digital Street Smarts

Just like you learn street smarts for staying safe in the real world, you need digital street smarts for staying safe online. Here's how to develop them:

### Trust Your Gut

If something feels wrong online - like a too-good-to-be-true offer or a creepy message - trust that feeling. Your instincts often pick up on warning signs before your conscious mind does. It's like when you feel something's not right in a situation at school or in your neighborhood - that same instinct works online.

### Stay Alert

Being alert online means paying attention to warning signs. Are your friends suddenly sending strange messages? Did a website's address change slightly? Is an app asking for permissions it shouldn't need? These could be signs of potential danger, just like seeing a car driving suspiciously slowly in your neighborhood would make you alert.

### Know Your Exits

Always know how to get out of uncomfortable online situations. This might mean knowing how to block someone, report inappropriate content, or quickly exit a website or app. It's like knowing where the emergency exits are in a building - you hope you never need them, but you should know where they are.

### Keep Learning

Digital threats change constantly, so staying safe means keeping up with new risks and safety measures. Follow trusted sources for online safety tips, talk to knowledgeable adults, and share what you learn with your friends. Think of it like learning new safety rules as you grow up - the rules you followed as a little kid aren't all the same ones you follow now.

## Conclusion

Remember, feeling safe online and actually being safe are two different things. The internet is an amazing place full of opportunities for learning, connecting, and having fun - but it requires awareness and careful navigation. By understanding the illusion of online safety, recognizing common misconceptions, learning from others' experiences, and developing your digital street smarts, you can better protect yourself while enjoying all the benefits the digital world has to offer.

## Coming Up Next

Get ready to dive into "Your Personal Information is Gold" in our next chapter! We'll explore why your personal information is so valuable, who might want it, and most importantly, how to protect it. You'll learn fascinating things about data collection and privacy that will change how you think about sharing information online. Plus, we'll share some cool tricks for keeping your personal information safe while still enjoying everything the internet has to offer. Stay tuned - your journey to becoming a digital safety expert continues!

# Your Thought on Online Safety Illusion

1. When do you feel most safe online? Are there times when this feeling of safety might be misleading?

2. What are three common myths about online safety that you used to believe? Why were they wrong?

3. Remember a time when you or someone you know felt too safe online. What happened?

# Did you know?

Your face is likely in dozens of strangers' photos! When people take pictures in public places like theme parks or tourist spots, you might accidentally be in the background. Some facial recognition databases already contain over 100 billion facial images!

# CHAPTER 3

## Your Personal Information is Precious

Photo: Adobe Photo Stock

Imagine your personal information as pieces of treasure - each piece might seem small and not very valuable on its own, but when put together, they create something incredibly precious. Just like gold miners search for valuable minerals, there are people and companies out there searching for your personal information. Let's discover why your data is so valuable and how you can protect your digital treasure!

# What is Personal Information?

Personal information is any data that can identify you or tell others about your life. Think of it like your digital DNA - it's unique to you and tells a story about who you are. Some personal information is obvious, like your name or address, but other types might surprise you. Let's explore the different kinds of personal information you might be sharing without even realizing it:

## Direct Identifiers:

These are the pieces of information that point directly to you, like your full name, home address, phone number, email address, or student ID number. Think of these as the keys to your digital house - you wouldn't give your house key to a stranger, and you should be just as careful with these pieces of information.

## Indirect Identifiers:

This is information that might not identify you immediately but could be used to figure out who you are. For example, your birthday, the school you attend, your favorite sports team, or the name of your pet might seem harmless to share, but when combined with other information, they can help someone identify you. It's like putting together pieces of a puzzle - each piece adds more detail to the picture.

## Behavioral Information:

This is data about what you do online - the websites you visit, the games you play, the videos you watch, and even how long you spend on different apps. It's like leaving footprints in the sand - every move you make online creates a trail that can tell others about your interests, habits, and preferences.

## Location Data:

Many apps and devices track where you are or where you've been. This includes not just your current location, but places you visit regularly, like your school, favorite hangout spots, or sports practice locations. Sharing location data is like drawing a map of your daily life for others to see.

## Why Do People Want Your Data?

Photo: Adobe Photo Stock

You might wonder why anyone would care about your personal information, especially if you're young. Well, there are several reasons why your data is valuable to different people and organizations:

### Companies and Marketers:

Businesses collect your data to understand what you like and don't like, so they can show you targeted advertisements. For example, if you've been watching videos about skateboarding, you might start seeing ads for skateboards and skating gear. It's like having a store clerk who remembers everything you've ever looked at and uses that information to suggest things you might want to buy.

### Game and App Developers:

They collect data about how you use their products to make them more addictive and to encourage you to spend money on in-app purchases. They might track when you play, what features you use most, and what makes you stop playing. It's similar to a candy company studying which flavors keep you coming back for more.

## Cybercriminals:

Bad actors want your personal information for various harmful purposes, such as identity theft, scams, or gaining access to your family's financial information. They might use details about your life to trick you or others into trusting them. Think of it like a burglar who learns your daily routine to know when you're not home.

## Data Brokers:

These are companies that collect and sell personal information. They gather data from many different sources to create detailed profiles about people, which they then sell to other companies. It's like someone following you around with a notebook, writing down everything you do, and then selling that information to others.

## The Data Collection Game

Photo: Adobe Photo Stock

Understanding how your data is collected is crucial for protecting it. Companies and websites use many clever techniques to gather information about you:

22

### Cookies and Tracking:

When you visit websites, they often place small files called "cookies" on your device. These cookies act like little spies that remember what you do on the site and sometimes follow you to other sites.

For example, if you look at shoes on one website, you might see ads for those same shoes on other websites you visit later.

### Social Media Mining:

Everything you do on social media can be collected and analyzed - your likes, shares, comments, and even how long you look at certain posts. The platforms use this information to keep you engaged and show you content they think you'll like. It's like having someone watch over your shoulder while you read a magazine, noting which articles interest you most.

### Games and Apps:

Many free games and apps make money by collecting and selling your data. They might ask for permissions they don't really need, like access to your contacts or photos. Some games even track things like your reaction time or decision-making patterns. It's similar to a friend letting you play with their toys but secretly recording everything you do with them.

### Connected Devices:

Smart devices, from phones to gaming consoles to smart speakers, can collect data about your habits and preferences. They might record what you say, when you're active, or what you ask them to do. Think of them as digital assistants who remember everything you tell them - and sometimes things you don't tell them directly.

## Privacy vs. Convenience

Photo: Adobe Photo Stock

One of the trickiest things about protecting your personal information is balancing privacy with convenience. Many apps and services offer helpful features in exchange for your data. Let's explore this trade-off:

### The Convenience Factor:

When you let apps access your location, they can give you directions, show nearby restaurants, or help you find your friends. When you allow websites to remember your login information, you don't have to type it in every time. These features make life easier, but they come at the cost of sharing more personal information.

### Making Smart Choices:

Instead of sharing everything or nothing, you can make smart choices about what to share and when. It's like choosing when to take shortcuts - sometimes the longer, more private way is safer.

For example, you might turn on location services only when you need directions, then turn them off again. Or you might use a password manager instead of letting websites save your login details.

## Setting Boundaries:

Just because an app or website asks for information doesn't mean you have to give it. Ask yourself: "Does this app really need this information to work?" For instance, a calculator app doesn't need access to your photos, and a drawing app doesn't need your location. Learning to say "no" to unnecessary data collection is an important skill.

# Your Rights in the Digital World

Photo: Adobe Photo Stock

You have important rights when it comes to your personal information, even as a young person. Understanding these rights helps you protect yourself better:

## The Right to Privacy:

Many countries have laws protecting your right to privacy, especially for young people. These laws often require companies to get permission from parents before collecting data from kids under a certain age. It's like having a bodyguard who makes sure others respect your personal space.

### The Right to Know:
You have the right to know what information companies are collecting about you and how they're using it. This is why websites have privacy policies (even though they're often hard to read!). You can usually ask companies to show you what data they have about you.

### The Right to Delete:
In many places, you have the right to ask companies to delete your personal information. This is sometimes called "the right to be forgotten." Think of it like being able to erase your footprints in the sand - though remember, some traces might still remain.

### The Right to Control:
You have the right to control how your information is used. This means you can often opt out of data collection or choose what information to share. Many apps and websites have privacy settings that let you control what you share and who can see it.

## Conclusion
Your personal information is incredibly valuable, and protecting it is an important life skill in our digital age. Remember that every piece of information you share online adds to your digital profile, and while sharing some information is necessary to enjoy online services, you should always think carefully about what you're sharing and why.

Just as you wouldn't give away real gold to strangers, you shouldn't give away your personal information without good reason. By understanding what personal information is, why it's valuable, how it's collected, and what rights you have, you can make better decisions about protecting your digital treasure.

## Coming Up Next
Get ready to dive into "The Cyber Threat Zoo" in our next chapter! We'll explore the different types of digital dangers that exist online, from sneaky viruses to clever scams. But don't worry - it's not about being scared; it's about being prepared! You'll learn how to spot these threats and, more importantly, how to protect yourself from them. Plus, we'll share some cool tools and

techniques that can help keep you safe while you enjoy your online adventures. Stay tuned - things are about to get really interesting!

# Your Thought on Personal Information Safety

4. What pieces of personal information have you shared online that might help someone create a profile about you?

5. Why do companies want your data? How do they use it to make money?

6. Would you trade your privacy for convenience? What apps have you given permissions to that might not really need them?

# Did you know?

Your personal data can be worth more than gold! While a gram of gold is worth around $60, the complete digital identity of a person can sell for up to $1,200 on the dark web. Cybercriminals particularly value children's data because it often goes unchecked for years!

# CHAPTER 4

## Cyber Threats

Photo: Adobe Photo Stock

Just like a real zoo has different types of animals, the digital world has different types of threats that we need to learn about. Don't worry though - once you know what these "digital animals" look like and how they behave, you'll be much better at keeping them away from your digital space. Let's explore these cyber creatures and learn how to stay safe from them!

## Understanding Different Types of Cyber Threats

Photo: Adobe Photo Stock

Online threats encompass a variety of malicious software and tactics aimed at compromising the security of computers and networks. These threats can result in data loss, financial theft, and unauthorized access to personal information. By recognizing different types of online threats, such as viruses, worms, and Trojans, users can better protect their systems and maintain their digital safety. Understanding these dangers is the first step in implementing effective preventive measures against them.

### Viruses

Think of computer viruses like the flu - they can spread from one device to another and make them "sick." A computer virus attaches itself to programs or files on your device, just like the flu virus attaches to cells in your body. When you open an infected file or program, the virus activates and can start causing problems. It might delete your files, slow down your device, or even break some of your programs.

### Worms

Worms are even sneakier than viruses because they don't need you to open anything to spread. They can crawl through network connections on their own, like actual worms tunneling through soil. Once a worm gets into one device on a network (like your home Wi-Fi), it can try to infect all the other connected devices too. Imagine if one person's cold could automatically spread to everyone in the house - that's kind of how computer worms work!

## Trojans

Trojans are named after the famous Trojan Horse from ancient Greece, and they work in a similar way. They pretend to be something helpful or fun, but they're actually hiding something dangerous inside. Trojans are like if someone gave you a box of candy, but inside was actually a box of bugs!

For example, you might download what looks like a cool new game, but hidden inside is a program that can steal your passwords or spy on what you're doing.

**Real World Example:** Tommy, age 13, downloaded what he thought was a free version of a popular game. Soon after, his computer started acting strange - programs opened by themselves, his homepage changed, and weird ads kept popping up. The "free game" was actually a Trojan that installed several viruses on his computer.

## Ransomware

Ransomware is like a digital kidnapper that locks up your files and demands money to give them back. Imagine if someone put a super-strong lock on your bedroom door and said you had to pay them to get back in - that's basically what ransomware does to your digital stuff. It encrypts (scrambles) your files so you can't open them, then demands payment (usually in cryptocurrency) to unscramble them.

**Real World Example:** James, age 14, clicked on what he thought was a download link for homework help. Suddenly, all his files were locked, and a message demanded $200 to unlock them. His family had to restore everything from backups, and James lost some recent photos and documents that hadn't been backed up.

## Spyware

Spyware is exactly what it sounds like - software that spies on you. It's like having an invisible person following you around, watching everything you do online. Spyware can track which websites you visit, record what you type (including passwords), and even turn on your camera or microphone without you knowing. Some spyware is designed to steal information, while other types try to figure out the best ways to show you ads.

## Phishing

Phishing is like digital fishing - criminals throw out "bait" (usually through emails or messages) and wait for someone to bite. The bait might be a message that looks like it's from your bank, a social media platform, or even a friend. These messages usually try to scare you or excite you into clicking a link or sharing private information.

For example, you might get a message saying "Your account will be deleted in 24 hours unless you verify your password!" or "Congratulations! You've won a free phone - click here to claim it!" These messages are designed to make you act quickly without thinking.

## Social Engineering

Social engineering is like being a digital detective - but for evil purposes. Criminals study your social media posts, figure out who your friends are, and learn about your interests. Then they use this information to trick you. Maybe they've learned you love a certain game, so they send you a message about a special offer for that game. Or they might pretend to be a friend of a friend who needs help.

## Identity Theft

Identity theft happens when someone pretends to be you online. They might use your name, pictures, or personal information to create fake accounts, buy things with your (or your parents') money, or trick other people. It's like someone stealing your student ID and pretending to be you at school - except online, it can be even harder to prove who's really you.

Criminals can piece together your identity from small bits of information you share in different places. Maybe you mentioned your birthday in one post, your pet's name in another, and your school in a third - put together, these details might help someone crack your passwords or answer your security questions.

## Cyberbullying

Cyberbullying is bullying that happens online, and it can be especially hurtful because it can happen anywhere, anytime. Unlike regular bullying that might stop when you leave school, cyberbullying can follow you home through your phone or computer. It might include mean messages, embarrassing photos being shared, fake accounts made to mock you, or getting excluded from online groups.

## Online Harassment

Online harassment goes beyond just being mean - it's a pattern of behavior meant to scare or upset you. This might include sending threatening messages, spreading rumors online, or encouraging others to gang up on you. Sometimes harassers might even try to find out where you live or go to school, which can be really scary.

## Identifying Cyber Threats

Photo: Adobe Photo Stock

Learning to identify digital threats is akin to the work of a skilled nature guide who can discern potentially dangerous animals in the wild. Just as a guide understands the signs and behaviors of wildlife, becoming adept at recognizing online risks takes time and experience. With diligent practice, one can learn to look for specific indicators that signal potential dangers. These warning signs may include unusual account activity, suspicious emails that seem off-brand, or unexpected requests for personal information. By honing your skills and staying vigilant, you can navigate the digital landscape more safely and effectively.

## Virus and Malware Warning Signs

In today's digital landscape, being vigilant about the health of your devices is more important than ever. Viruses and malware can silently infiltrate your system, leading to degraded performance, privacy breaches, and potential data loss. Understanding the warning signs can empower you to take action before significant damage occurs. Here are some common indicators that your device may have been compromised.

### Your Device Becomes Unusually Slow

Imagine your device as a person overloaded with heavy bags—this can happen when it's affected by viruses or malware. Infected devices experience sluggishness because harmful programs operate in the background, using valuable system resources. If you notice that your once speedy tablet is now struggling to open games or switching between apps feels like wading through molasses, it's time to investigate.

### Programs Launching Spontaneously

It's as if a mischievous ghost has infiltrated your device! If you find applications opening without your command, or if your web browser is unexpectedly redirecting to strange websites, you could be dealing with malware. For instance, when Lisa noticed her laptop repeatedly opening the calculator app and unfamiliar games, it was a clear alert that her machine had been infected.

### Unexplained Changes to Your Homepage

Imagine returning home to find your furniture rearranged without your consent; that's what it feels like when your browser's homepage changes unexpectedly. If you notice your default search engine has been swapped for one you don't recognize, or if there are new toolbars installed without your knowledge, it might be a sign of malware interference. These changes can disrupt your browsing experience and compromise your online security.

## Intrusive Pop-up Advertisements

Think of pop-up ads as unwanted guests who just won't leave. If you're bombarded by persistent ads, even when you're not actively browsing online, it's time to worry. Particularly concerning are ads that appear inappropriate or overly explicit, alongside pop-ups suggesting that your device is infected and urgently needs cleaning. Most of these messages are scams designed to trick you into taking harmful actions.

## Mysterious Changes to Files

This situation is akin to someone sneaking into your room and relocating your belongings. If you notice files appearing on your desktop that you didn't create, or if your significant documents seem to disappear or get altered without your approval, you may have a malware issue. Additionally, if your friends receive strange messages from you, it could indicate that malware is leveraging your accounts to spread further.

By identifying these warning signs early, you can safeguard your devices and personal information against potentially harmful threats. Take action right away if you suspect your device may be compromised!

## Phishing and Scam Red Flags:

Photo: Adobe Photo Stock

In a digital world increasingly fraught with deception and fraud, recognizing the warning signs of phishing and scams is essential for protecting your personal and financial information. Phishing and scam red flags are indicators that a communication—be it an email, text, or message—may originate from malicious sources attempting to deceive you. Being vigilant and informed can help you navigate online interactions safely and avoid falling victim to these scams. This guide will outline key characteristics to watch for, empowering you to identify potential threats before they lead to dire consequences.

### Urgent and Alarmist Messages
Scammers often create a sense of urgency to provoke hasty decisions, leaving you little time to think critically. Look out for messages that pressure you with phrases like "Your account will be deleted in 24 hours! Act immediately!" or "Urgent security alert—click here right now!" Such tactics are designed to provoke panic and compel you to act without reasoning.

### Offers That Sound Too Good to Be True
Be wary of messages promising improbable rewards or offers that seem

unbelievable. If you receive claims like "You've won a luxurious vacation!" or "Earn $1,000 a day from the comfort of your home!" proceed with caution. These enticing offers often mask intentions to exploit your personal information or finances.

## Spelling and Grammar Errors

Professional organizations typically maintain high standards of communication. Be on guard for emails rife with multiple spelling and grammar mistakes, which are common in scams. Watch for unusual phrasing or a blend of formal and casual language that feels out of place—it may indicate a scammer's attempt to impersonate a legitimate entity.

## Deceptive Links and URLs

Authentic links are crucial for secure online interactions. Scammers often create URL obfuscations that appear similar to legitimate web addresses but contain slight discrepancies. Examples include "paypa1.com" instead of "paypal.com" or "googgle.com" instead of "google.com." Always hover over links (without clicking!) to reveal their true destination before proceeding.

## Requests for Sensitive Personal Information

Be highly skeptical of any unsolicited requests for personal or financial information via email or messages. Legitimate companies like banks or service providers rarely ask for sensitive information—such as passwords, PINs, or full credit card numbers—through insecure channels.

## Uncharacteristic Behavior from Friends

If you receive messages from friends that seem out of character—such as unusual writing styles, strange requests for money, or links sent without context—this may indicate their account has been compromised. Pay attention to the nuances of their usual communication patterns to distinguish between a genuine conversation and a potential scam attempt.

**Real World Example:** Maria, age 12, got an email saying she'd won a new tablet in a contest she never entered. All she had to do was click a link and enter her address for shipping. Luckily, she remembered learning about phishing in school and showed the email to her mom instead. They discovered it was a scam trying to collect personal information.

## Identity Theft Warning Signs:

Photo: Adobe Photo Stock

In this hyper-connected digital world, safeguarding your personal information has become more crucial than ever before. Identity theft can have devastating effects, leaving victims feeling violated and anxious. Recognizing the warning signs of identity theft is essential for taking swift and effective action. By being vigilant and informed, you can protect your personal information, financial stability, and overall peace of mind. The following indicators serve as crucial signals that your identity may be compromised, urging you to investigate further and secure your digital presence.

## Unexpected Account Notifications

Receiving unexpected alerts about accounts linked to your personal information can be alarming. These may include password reset requests or welcome emails for accounts you never created. Such notifications signal potential unauthorized access to your information, making it vital to examine your online security.

## Unauthorized Posts and Messages

Discovering unfamiliar posts or messages on your social media accounts can be deeply unsettling. This breach not only misrepresents your online persona but also raises concerns about how these actions might affect your relationships and reputation. It's crucial to monitor your accounts regularly to maintain control over your online identity.

## Confusing Requests from Friends

When friends reach out, confused by strange messages or friend requests that seem to originate from you, it can damage trust and lead to misunderstanding. These interactions may indicate that someone is misusing your account, underscoring the importance of protecting your identity and reassuring your social circle.

## Unrecognized Purchases

Encountering unfamiliar transactions on your financial statements can trigger alarm bells about your financial security. This could suggest unauthorized access to your accounts, making it imperative to scrutinize your financial activities and take quick action to secure your assets.

## Unsolicited Password Change Emails

Receiving unexpected emails about password changes that you did not initiate can provoke anxiety and fear. These communications are often indicators of a potential security breach, emphasizing the necessity to strengthen your online protections and regain control over your accounts.

**Real World Example:** Alex, age 15, noticed someone had created a fake account using his photos and was messaging his friends asking for gift card codes. Instead of panicking, he: 1) Reported the fake account, 2) Warned his friends through a different platform, 3) Changed all his passwords, and 4) Told his parents. His quick action prevented anyone from falling for the scam.

## Experiencing Cyberbullying and Harassment:

Photo: Adobe Photo Stock

Experiencing cyberbullying and harassment involves a range of distressing behaviors that can significantly impact an individual's mental and emotional health. This includes receiving a barrage of threatening messages, having personal information shared without consent, and facing social exclusion from online groups. The creation of fake accounts for mockery can damage self-esteem, while unsettling messages can instill fear and anxiety. Overall, these harmful actions foster a sense of vulnerability and isolation, underscoring the urgent need for awareness and intervention in the digital space. Let's discuss these concepts in detail:

### Receiving a barrage of mean or threatening messages

This can involve an ongoing series of hostile texts, emails, or social media posts aimed directly at you, often featuring harsh language, insults, or direct threats. Such communications can foster a sense of fear and anxiety, significantly impacting your emotional health.

### Having personal information or pictures shared without consent

This refers to instances where private aspects of your life, like confidential messages, location details, or personal images, are unlawfully disseminated without your approval. This breach of privacy can lead to feelings of vulnerability and distress, as your trust is violated and your personal space infringed upon.

### Being left out of online groups or games

Exclusion can occur when you are intentionally omitted from online conversations, activities, or gaming events. This social isolation can be particularly painful, as it may elicit feelings of rejection and inadequacy, resulting in a reduced sense of belonging within your digital communities.

### The creation of fake accounts for amusement

This involves the establishment of impersonating profiles or parody accounts that mock or demean you, often utilizing distorted images or fabricated claims. Such actions can greatly affect your self-esteem and might harm your reputation within your social circles.

### Receiving unsettling and frightening messages

These communications can take various forms, including cryptic threats, disturbing remarks, or inappropriate content meant to alarm or agitate you. Experiencing such messages can lead to increased feelings of anxiety and fear, as you may feel threatened or targeted in your online exchanges.

**Real World Example:** Sofia, age 13, started getting mean comments on all her social media posts from an anonymous account. The account seemed to know personal details about her life, and she suspected it was someone from school. She felt scared to post anything online. After talking to her parents and school counselor, they were able to report and block the account, and Sofia learned new ways to protect her privacy online.

### Conclusion

The Cyber Threat Zoo might seem scary, but remember - just like real animals, cyber threats are usually more afraid of prepared people than prepared people are of them! By understanding what these threats are, how they work, and how to spot them, you're already much safer. Remember that it's not about being perfect or never making mistakes - it's about being aware, staying cautious, and knowing what to do if you encounter a threat.

The best protection is knowledge and preparation. Keep your digital security tools (like antivirus software) updated, think before you click or share, and always trust your instincts if something feels wrong. And most importantly, never be afraid to ask for help from a trusted adult if you encounter something suspicious or scary online.

## Coming Up Next

Get ready for "Social Media Safety" in our next chapter! We'll dive into the exciting world of social media and learn how to have fun while staying safe. You'll discover cool tricks for protecting your privacy, managing your online reputation, and dealing with awkward or uncomfortable situations on social platforms. Plus, we'll share some awesome tips for creating a positive digital footprint that you'll be proud of later. Stay tuned - it's time to become a social media safety expert!

# Your Understanding about Cyber Threats

1. How would you explain the difference between a virus, worm, and Trojan to your friends?

2. What warning signs have you noticed on your own devices that might indicate a security problem?

3. If you discovered malware on your device tomorrow, what steps would you take?

# Did you know?

The first computer virus was actually created by a father for his children! Called "Elk Cloner," it was written by 15-year-old Rich Skrenta in 1982 as a joke and spread via Apple II computers through floppy disks. It simply displayed a poem on infected computers!

# CHAPTER 5

## Social Media Safety

Photo: Adobe Photo Stock

Welcome to the world of social media! Whether you're sharing dance videos on TikTok, posting photos on Instagram, chatting with friends on Snapchat, or connecting with classmates on other platforms, social media can be super fun and creative. But just like a swimming pool needs safety rules to keep everyone safe while having fun, social media needs some safety guidelines too. Let's dive into how you can enjoy social media while protecting yourself!

## Platform-Specific Safety Tips

Photo: Adobe Photo Stock

Each social media platform is like a different neighborhood with its own culture and safety considerations. Let's explore how to stay safe on the most popular platforms:

### Instagram Safety

Instagram is all about sharing photos and videos, but it's important to control who sees your content. First, consider making your account private - this means only people you approve can see your posts. Think of it like having a guest list for your birthday party; you get to choose who's invited! Don't accept follow requests from people you don't know in real life, even if they seem to have mutual friends with you.

Watch out for Instagram DMs (direct messages) from strangers, especially those with business opportunities or modeling offers - these are often scams. If someone you don't know sends you a message, it's best to ignore it or block them. Remember, Instagram has a feature that filters message requests, keeping suspicious ones in a separate folder.

## Facebook Safety

Facebook is like a big digital neighborhood where it's easy to share too much information. Start by adjusting your privacy settings so only friends can see your posts. Remember, your profile picture and cover photo are usually public, so choose these carefully. Use Facebook's Privacy Checkup tool (the little dinosaur guide) to review all your settings.

Watch out for friend suggestions - just because Facebook says you have "mutual friends" doesn't mean you should accept the request. A good rule is: if you wouldn't say hi to this person in real life, don't friend them online. For Facebook Groups, keep an eye on their privacy settings; some groups automatically make your membership public, which means anyone can see you're a member.

Facebook Messenger needs special attention too. Use the "Message Request" folder to screen messages from people you don't know, and consider turning off your "Active Status" so people can't see when you're online.

## TikTok Security

TikTok is fun for creating and sharing videos, but it can expose you to strangers if you're not careful. Use TikTok's Family Pairing feature if your parents want to help manage your safety settings. Keep your account private until you're old enough and experienced enough to handle public posting.

Be extra careful with the music you use and the dances you perform - some content might seem innocent but could attract the wrong kind of attention. Also, think twice before participating in challenges. Ask yourself: "Would I feel comfortable if my grandparents saw this video?" If the answer is no, maybe reconsider posting it.

## Snapchat Security

Remember that even though Snapchat messages and photos "disappear," people can still screenshot them or record their screen. Never send anything you wouldn't want saved forever. Be especially careful with Snap Map - consider using "Ghost Mode" so others can't see your location.

For friend requests on Snapchat, only accept people you know in real life. The

"Quick Add" feature might suggest friends-of-friends, but that doesn't mean they're safe to add. Think of it like this: just because someone knows your friend doesn't mean you'd invite them to your house!

## YouTube Safety

YouTube is like a giant TV station where anyone can be a broadcaster, but not all content is kid-friendly. First, make sure you're using YouTube while signed into an age-appropriate account - this helps filter out inappropriate content. If you make videos, consider keeping them "Unlisted" so only people with the link can see them, or "Private" so only specific people can watch.

Be extra careful with comments - both ones you receive and ones you make. Remember that comments are public and can be seen by anyone. Never share personal information in comments or video descriptions. If you're a content creator, learn to use YouTube's moderation tools to filter out inappropriate comments.

For live streams, be careful about showing your surroundings or sharing personal details during the stream. Consider using a virtual background if you're showing yourself on camera.

## WeChat Safety

WeChat combines many features like messaging, social media, and payments, which means extra care is needed. Use the privacy settings to control who can add you as a contact - setting it to "Friends Only" or requiring a QR code is safest. Be careful with WeChat Moments (their version of a social feed) - adjust who can see your posts and consider creating custom groups for sharing different types of content.

Never share your WeChat Pay or banking information with anyone, even if they claim to be from WeChat support. Be cautious with WeChat's "People Nearby" feature - it's best to keep this turned off to prevent strangers from finding you.

## Telegram Safety

Telegram is known for its security features, but you still need to be careful. Use Telegram's privacy settings to control who can see your phone number, last seen status, and profile photos. Be especially careful with Telegram groups and channels - some may contain inappropriate content or scams.

The "Secret Chat" feature offers extra security with end-to-end encryption, but remember that people can still screenshot your messages. Don't join random groups through links, and be careful about using Telegram's "People Nearby" feature - it's safer to keep it disabled.

## Reddit Safety

Reddit is like a huge collection of topic-based clubs (subreddits), but it requires careful navigation. Create a username that doesn't reveal anything about your real identity. Be careful about what you share in comments - people can look through your comment history to piece together information about you.

Never share personal information, even if someone claims to be hosting a contest or offering a prize. Be especially careful with direct messages - Reddit's chat feature can be used by anyone unless you adjust your privacy settings. Consider turning off the option to receive chat requests and direct messages from strangers.

## Discord Safety

Discord is popular for gaming and community chat, but it needs strong safety settings. Start by adjusting your privacy settings:

- Turn off the ability for anyone to add you as a friend
- Only accept direct messages from server members you've explicitly approved
- Be careful about joining random servers through invite links

For each server you join, review the server-specific privacy settings. Be cautious about sharing personal information, even in seemingly private channels. Remember that server administrators can see everything posted in their servers.

## Pinterest Safety

While Pinterest might seem harmless since it's mostly about sharing images, it still needs privacy consideration. Set your profile to private if you don't want others to see what you're saving. Be careful about boards that might reveal too much personal information (like "My Dream Home" with your address or "My Birthday Wishlist" with personal details).

Watch out for scam pins that lead to fake websites, especially those promising free products or amazing deals. When creating boards about personal events or interests, consider making them "Secret" so only you can see them.

## Privacy Settings Made Simple

Photo: Adobe Photo Stock

Privacy settings are like the locks and security system for your digital house. Let's make them simple to understand and use:

### Basic Privacy Checkup

Begin by conducting a thorough privacy checkup on each of your social media accounts, focusing on essential settings that dictate your privacy. Start with who can see your posts and adjust the settings to ensure that only those you trust—such as friends and family—have access to your content. Next, examine the options for who can contact you through direct messages or friend requests, limiting these interactions to people you know or friends of friends to reduce unwanted outreach. It's also vital to review your search settings, ensuring that your profile cannot be easily found by strangers through email addresses or phone numbers. Finally, scrutinize the visibility of your personal information, such as your bio and profile details, to ensure that sensitive data remains private and is not publicly accessible. By addressing these key areas, you can significantly bolster your online privacy and safeguard your personal information from unwanted exposure.

## Advance Privacy Features

Many platforms now provide advanced privacy features that are essential for safeguarding your online presence. Utilizing two-factor authentication adds an extra layer of security, akin to having both a lock and an alarm system for your home. Additionally, setting up login alerts can notify you if someone attempts to access your account from an unfamiliar device, enabling prompt action to protect your information. You can also manage your activity status, allowing you to decide whether others can see when you're online, which can enhance your privacy. Finally, controlling who sees your stories or posts ensures that your temporary content reaches only the intended audience, giving you greater command over your digital interactions. By leveraging these features, you can significantly bolster your privacy and security online.

It is essential to regularly review your privacy settings on all platforms, as they frequently update their features and policies. Staying informed about these changes can help you protect your personal information and ensure that your preferences are in line with the current options available. Establish a routine to check your settings every few months, and take the time to understand any new features or adjustments made by the platform. This proactive approach will help you maintain your desired level of privacy and security.

## Think Before You Post

Photo: Adobe Photo Stock

Every post you make is like throwing a boomerang - it might come back to you someday! Before sharing anything online, pause and ask yourself these questions:

### The Future Test

Imagine yourself five years from now. Would you be happy to see this post? Remember, future schools, employers, or even friends might see what you share today. A silly post might seem funny now but could be embarrassing or problematic later.

### The Stranger Test

If a stranger saw this post, what could they learn about you? Could they figure out where you live, what school you go to, or what your daily routine is? Be careful not to share details that could help someone track you down in real life.

### The Screenshot Test

Always assume anything you post could be screenshot and shared, even if it's supposed to be temporary. Would you be okay if someone saved this content and showed it to others? Remember, once something is online, you lose control over who might eventually see it.

## Location Services and Tagging

Location sharing on social media is like giving someone a map to find you. While it might seem fun to check in at places or tag your location in posts, this information can be dangerous in the wrong hands.

## Smart Location Sharing

Instead of sharing your location in real-time, consider posting about places after you've left. This way, you can share your experiences without telling everyone where to find you.

For example, rather than checking in at the movie theater while you're there, post about the movie after you're home.

## Tagging Tips

Be thoughtful about tagging others in your posts - always ask permission first. Just like you wouldn't want someone sharing your location without asking, don't do it to others. This includes tagging friends in photos, checking them in at locations, or mentioning them in posts.

## Dealing with Unwanted Attention

Photo: Adobe Photo Stock

Sometimes you might get attention from people you'd rather not interact with online. Here's how to handle different situations:

### Unwanted Friend Requests

If you get friend requests from strangers, it's okay to ignore or decline them. You don't owe anyone an explanation for not wanting to connect. If someone keeps sending requests after you've declined, most platforms allow you to block them completely.

### Harassment and Bullying

Always tell a trusted adult if you're being harassed online. You don't have to deal with this alone! If someone is bothering you online, remember the three-step approach:

1. Don't respond - engaging often makes things worse
2. Document everything - take screenshots of harmful messages or posts
3. Report and block - use the platform's reporting tools and block the person

## Photo and Video Sharing Safety

Photos and videos can reveal more than you might realize. Here's how to share safely:

## Background Check

Before posting photos or videos, check the background for details that might give away personal information. Is your school visible? Can someone see your house number? Are there any private documents or screens visible? Take a moment to scan for these details before sharing.

## Clothing and Content

Make sure your photos and videos show you in appropriate clothing and situations. A good rule is: if you wouldn't wear it to school, don't post it online. Also be mindful of gestures, poses, or actions that might be misinterpreted or inappropriate.

## Sharing Rules

Create personal rules for what you will and won't share. For example:

- No photos in school uniforms that show the school name
- No pictures of house keys or credit cards (even partially visible)
- No photos of official documents or tickets with barcodes
- No sharing other people's photos without permission

## Conclusion

Social media can be an amazing way to connect with friends, express yourself, and share your interests with others. By following these safety guidelines, you can enjoy all the fun parts of social media while protecting yourself from potential risks. Remember, it's not about being afraid to use social media - it's about using it wisely and safely.

Think of these safety practices like wearing a seatbelt in a car - they don't stop you from going anywhere, but they keep you protected while you're on your journey. Keep checking your privacy settings, think before you post, and always trust your instincts if something doesn't feel right.

## Coming Up Next

Get ready to level up your gaming safety in our next chapter, "Gaming World Safety"! We'll explore how to have epic gaming adventures while protecting yourself from online predators, scams, and toxic behavior. You'll learn about securing your gaming accounts, managing in-game purchases safely, and dealing with different types of players you might meet in your favorite games. Whether you're a casual player or a serious gamer, you won't want to miss these essential tips for staying safe while having fun in virtual worlds!

# Your Thought on Social Media Safety

1. Review your social media privacy settings. What surprised you most about what others can see?

2. How do you decide who to accept as a friend or follower online? What's your process?

3. What would you do if a friend shared an embarrassing photo of you without permission?

# Did you know?

Social media platforms can predict your future behavior with 93% accuracy just by analyzing your likes! They can determine your personality traits, political views, and even your future career choices before you've made them yourself.

# CHAPTER 6

## Gaming World Safety

Photo: Adobe Photo Stock

Ready, player? Whether you're building worlds in Minecraft, battling in Fortnite, hanging out in Roblox, or exploring other amazing game universes, online gaming can be incredibly fun and exciting. But just like any adventure, you need the right equipment and knowledge to stay safe. Let's level up your gaming safety skills!

## Online Gaming Risks

Photo: Adobe Photo Stock

The gaming world is like a massive multiplayer adventure, but not everyone playing is there just to have fun. Some players might try to scam you, steal your account information, or even attempt to gather personal information about you. Understanding these risks is your first power-up in staying safe!

### Account Theft

Account theft in gaming is more common than you might think, and losing an account you've spent months or years building can be devastating. Imagine spending countless hours leveling up your character, collecting rare items, or building amazing structures, only to have someone steal it all away. Hackers might try to get your login information through fake websites that promise free in-game items or currency. They might also attempt to trick you by pretending to be game moderators or support staff.

### Personal Information Risks

Some players might try to piece together information about you from what you share while gaming. They might start with casual questions about your age or where you live, then gradually ask for more specific details. Think of it like a puzzle - each piece of information you share is another clue about who you are and where to find you. Even sharing seemingly harmless details like your school mascot or your pet's name could help someone guess your passwords or security questions.

## Financial Risks

Gaming involves more financial risks than just unauthorized purchases. Some scammers create fake gaming markets or trading sites that steal your payment information. Others might offer to sell you in-game items at amazing prices, take your money, and disappear. There are even cases where scammers convince young players to share their parents' credit card information for "exclusive" game items.

## In-Game Purchases and Microtransactions

Understanding how to handle in-game purchases safely is crucial in today's gaming world. Many games are "free to play" but make money through small purchases for things like character skins, special items, or game currency.

## Understanding the Real Cost

Photo: Adobe Photo Stock

That cool skin might only cost a few dollars, but these small purchases can add up quickly. Think of it like buying snacks - each candy bar might not cost much, but buying one every day adds up to a lot of money by the end of the month. Many games use special currencies (like V-Bucks in Fortnite or Robux in Roblox) to make it harder to track how much real money you're spending. Always remember that even though you're using "game money," it's still real money being spent.

## Setting Boundaries

It's important to have clear rules about in-game purchases. Talk with your parents about whether you can make purchases, how much you can spend, and what kind of items you can buy. Some families set up a gaming budget or require permission before any purchase. This isn't about limiting fun - it's about learning to make smart decisions with money, even in virtual worlds.

## Avoiding Purchase Scams

Be extremely careful about offers for "free" game currency or items. If someone promises to give you free V-Bucks, Robux, or other game currency, it's almost certainly a scam. These scams might ask you to:

- Complete surveys
- Download suspicious apps
- Share your account information
- Click on links to "claim your prize"

Remember: If it seems too good to be true, it probably is a scam!

## Chat Safety While Gaming

Photo: Adobe Photo Stock

Game chat can be a fun way to strategize with teammates or make new friends, but it needs careful handling to stay safe. Whether you're using voice chat or text chat, following some key safety rules can help protect you from harmful situations.

### Voice Chat Safety

Voice chat adds excitement to games but can also reveal more about you than you intend. Your voice can give away your age and gender, and background noises might reveal things about your location or home life. Consider using voice changers for public games, or limit voice chat to friends you know in real life. Never feel pressured to use voice chat if you're not comfortable - many successful gamers only use text chat or quick commands.

### Text Chat Wisdom

Text chat might seem safer than voice chat, but it comes with its own risks. People might try to start private conversations that gradually become inappropriate. They might share links to dangerous websites or try to move the conversation to other platforms where there's less monitoring. Remember that once something is typed in chat, you can't control who might see it or screenshot it.

## What to Share and What to Keep Private
Create clear rules for yourself about what you will and won't share in-game chat. Although you can share game strategies and tips, make general comments about the game, and send basic reactions and celebrations. However, it is crucial to conceal your real name or age, where you live or go to school, when you're home alone, your personal problems or feelings, and other family information.

# Protecting Your Gaming Accounts
Your gaming account is like a digital treasure chest containing your achievements, items, and sometimes financial information. Protecting it should be a top priority!

## Strong Password Protection
Create a unique, strong password for each of your gaming accounts. Never use the same password across different games or platforms. A good gaming password should combine:

- o   Your favorite game character
- o   A random number sequence
- o   Special characters
- o   Capital and lowercase letters

For example, "Mario123" is a weak password, but "SuperM@rio2847Jump!" is much stronger.

## Two-Factor Authentication
Think of two-factor authentication (2FA) as adding a second lock to your account. Even if someone guesses your password, they still can't get in without the second key (usually a code sent to your phone or email). Enable 2FA on every platform that offers it – it is like having a security guard checking IDs at the door.

## Account Recovery Options
Set up account recovery options carefully. This includes;

o   secure email address (which you have access to),

o   recovery phone numbers (with parent permission),

o   security questions (with answers only you would know), and

o   backup codes stored in a safe place.

## Dealing with Toxic Players

Photo: Adobe Photo Stock

Unfortunately, not everyone in the gaming world plays nice. Toxic players can try to ruin the fun through harassment, bullying, or inappropriate behavior. Learning to handle these situations is an important gaming skill.

### Recognizing Toxic Behavior

Toxic behavior in games can manifest in various ways, including verbal abuse in chat or voice communications, intentionally sabotaging gameplay for others, harassment or bullying, inappropriate language or content, and threats or intimidation. It's important to differentiate between competitive play and toxic behavior; playing hard to win is not the same as being deliberately harmful to others.

## Response Strategies

When dealing with toxic players, remember BLOCK:

B - Breathe and stay calm

L - Leave the situation if necessary

O - Only respond if you must, and keep it neutral

C - Capture evidence (screenshots, recordings)

K - Keep reporting tools handy

## Using Reporting Tools

Most games have built-in systems for reporting bad behavior. Learn how to use these tools in your favorite games. Good reports include:

- o Specific details about what happened
- o Screenshots or recordings if possible
- o Time and date of the incident
- o The toxic player's username
- o Any witnesses who saw what happened

## Building a Positive Gaming Environment

You can contribute to a better gaming community by being a good sport yourself and supporting new players. Speak out against toxic behavior when it is safe to do so, and play with friends who share your values. Join communities that actively moderate against toxicity to help create the positive change you want to see.

## Conclusion

Gaming should be fun, exciting, and safe! By understanding the risks, protecting your accounts, being smart about purchases, and knowing how to handle toxic behavior, you can enjoy all the amazing experiences gaming has to offer while staying safe.

Remember, being a smart gamer doesn't mean being a suspicious or unfriendly one. It means knowing how to protect yourself while still having great adventures and making new friends. Keep these safety tips in mind, and you'll be well-equipped to handle whatever challenges come your way in the gaming world.

## Coming Up Next

Get ready to become a master of your digital defense in our next chapter, "Password Power"! We'll explore the secrets of creating super-strong passwords that are hard to crack but easy to remember. You'll learn about password managers, two-factor authentication, and other cool tools that can help keep your digital life secure. Whether you're protecting your gaming accounts, social media, or school email, these password tips will help you level up your security game!

# Your Perception about Gaming World safety

1. What in-game purchases have you made or been tempted to make? Were they worth it?

2. How do you handle toxic players in your favorite games? Share your strategies.

3. What personal information might you accidentally reveal while gaming with strangers?

# Did you know?

Some online games employ full-time economists to manage their virtual economies! Games like EVE Online have their own financial systems so complex that scientists study them to understand real-world economic patterns.

# CHAPTER 7

## Password Power

Photo: Adobe Photo Stock

Think of passwords as the keys to your digital life. Just like you need different keys for your house, your bike lock, and your locker, you need different passwords for your various online accounts. But unlike physical keys, passwords can be much more powerful – if you know how to create and use them properly. Let's unlock the secrets of password power!

## Creating Super-Strong Passwords

Creating a strong password is like building a fortress around your digital accounts. Many people make the mistake of using simple passwords like "password123" or their birthday, which is like leaving their front door wide open! A truly strong password is like having multiple locks, security cameras, and a moat all protecting your castle. Let's learn how to create passwords that even the cleverness hackers would have trouble cracking.

## The Password Recipe

Think of creating a strong password like following a secret recipe. You need different ingredients that work together to make something powerful. A super-strong password should include:

First, start with a base phrase that means something to you but wouldn't be obvious to others. For example, instead of using your dog's name "Buddy," you might think of a funny moment like "BuddyAteMyHomework." This is just your starting point – we're going to make it even stronger!

Next, add some special characters to replace letters. Maybe the 'a' becomes '@' and the 'e' becomes '3'. Now we have "Buddy@t3MyHom3work". See how it's getting harder to guess but still makes sense to you?

Finally, add some random numbers that mean something to you. Maybe you won 1st place in a race on May 4th – add "1st54" to create "Buddy@t3MyHom3work1st54". This password is now like a fortress with multiple layers of security!

## Memorable Yet Strong

The trick to creating strong passwords is making them meaningful to you but nonsensical to others. Instead of using obvious personal information like your birthday or pet's name, create a password based on a story or memory.

For example: "My first home run was on field 7 in the rain" could become "1stHRf7inR@in!"

Think about a favorite book, movie quote, or song lyric, but mix it up in a way that only makes sense to you. "The wizard gave Harry his first letter" might become "WizG@veH-1stL3tter!" It's like creating a secret code that tells a story only you know.

## Password Manager Basics

Photo: Adobe Photo Stock

A password manager is like having a super-secure digital safe for all your passwords. Imagine trying to remember 20 or 30 different complex passwords – it's nearly impossible! That's where password managers come in to save the day.

### How Password Managers Work

Password managers are special programs that securely store all your passwords in one place. Think of it like a magical vault that only opens with one special key (your master password). Once inside, you can access all your other passwords whenever you need them. The best part? The password manager can even create super-strong passwords for you and remember them, so you don't have to!

### Choosing a Password Manager

When picking a password manager, look for one that:

1. Has a strong reputation for security

2. Works on all your devices (phone, tablet, computer)
3. Makes it easy to add and update passwords
4. Includes features like password generation and security alerts

Popular options include LastPass (with family plans), Bitwarden (which has a free version), and 1Password. Talk to your parents about choosing one that works for the whole family.

## Setting Up Your Digital Vault

Photo: Adobe Photo Stock

Setting up a password manager is like building your own secure vault. First, you'll create a master password – this needs to be the strongest password you've ever made because it protects all your other passwords! Write this password down and keep it somewhere super safe at home, or share it with a parent for safekeeping.

Then, start adding your existing passwords to the vault. As you do this, the password manager will probably tell you which passwords are weak and need to be updated. It's like having a security advisor checking your defenses!

## Two-Factor Authentication Made Easy

Two-factor authentication (2FA) is like having a second lock on your door. Even if someone figures out your password, they still can't get in without the second key. Let's make this important security feature easy to understand and use!

## Understanding 2FA

Imagine you're entering a top-secret clubhouse. First, you need to know the password (something you know), but then you also need to show your special club badge (something you have) before you can enter. That's how 2FA works – it requires two different types of proof that you are who you say you are.

## Different Types of 2FA

There are several ways to provide that second factor of authentication:

- Text message codes (though these aren't the most secure option)
- Authentication apps (like Google Authenticator or Authy)
- Security keys (small devices you plug into your computer)
- Biometric data (fingerprints or face recognition)

Think of these as different types of keys for your second lock. Some are stronger than others, but any 2FA is better than none!

## Setting Up 2FA

Setting up 2FA might seem complicated at first, but it's actually pretty simple. Most services will walk you through the process step by step. The most important thing is to keep your backup codes safe – these are like spare keys that let you get into your account if you lose access to your regular 2FA method.

## Biometric Security

Photo: Adobe Photo Stock

Biometric security is like having a lock that only opens for you – literally! Instead of typing a password, you can use unique features of your body, like your fingerprint or face, to unlock your devices and accounts.

### How Biometrics Work

Your fingerprint is like a one-of-a-kind pattern that nature gave only to you. When you set up fingerprint recognition on your phone or tablet, the device creates a special digital map of your fingerprint. Every time you try to unlock the device, it compares your finger to that map to make sure it's really you.

Face recognition works similarly, creating a detailed map of your facial features. It's like having a super-smart security guard who knows exactly what you look like and won't be fooled by a photograph or someone who looks similar to you.

### Advantages and Limitations

Biometric security is super convenient – you always have your fingerprint or face with you, and no one can steal them like they could steal a password. However, biometrics shouldn't be your only security measure. Think of them as an additional layer of protection, like having both a strong lock and a security camera.

## Password DO's and DON'Ts

Let's break down the most important rules for password security in a way that's easy to remember and follow. Think of these as your password power commandments!

### Password DO's

DO use different passwords for every account. This is like having different keys for different locks – if someone steals one key, they can't open everything.

- DO make your passwords long and complex. The longer and more random a password is, the harder it is to crack. Aim for at least 12 characters.
- DO use a mix of different types of characters. Combine uppercase and lowercase letters, numbers, and special characters to create stronger passwords.
- DO change your passwords if you think an account might have been compromised. This is like changing the locks if you lose your keys.
- DO use a password manager to keep track of all your passwords securely. It's much safer than writing them down or trying to remember them all.

### Password DON'Ts

DON'T share your passwords with anyone (except maybe your parents). Even if your best friend promises to keep it secret, sharing passwords is never a good idea.

- DON'T use personal information in your passwords. Your birthday, pet's name, or favorite team are too easy for others to guess.
- DON'T use the same password everywhere. If one account gets hacked, all your accounts could be at risk.
- DON'T save passwords in your browser without using a password

manager. Browser password storage isn't as secure as a dedicated password manager.

- DON'T write passwords down and leave them where others might find them. If you must write them down, keep them in a very safe place.

## Conclusion

Your passwords are the guardians of your digital life, protecting everything from your gaming accounts to your private messages. By creating strong passwords, using a password manager, enabling two-factor authentication, and following good password practices, you're building a powerful security system that helps keep your digital world safe.

Remember, good password security isn't about making things difficult for yourself – it's about making things difficult for the bad guys while keeping them manageable for you. With the right tools and habits, you can have both security and convenience.

## Coming Up Next

Get ready to become a device security expert in our next chapter, "Device Defense"! We'll explore how to protect all your devices – from smartphones to tablets to computers – from various threats. You'll learn about antivirus software, safe downloading practices, and how to keep your devices running smoothly and securely. Plus, we'll share some cool tricks for protecting your privacy while using public Wi-Fi. Stay tuned – your journey to becoming a digital security master continues!

# Your Believe About Password Strength

1. Without sharing your actual passwords, how strong do you think your current passwords are?

2. What's your strategy for remembering different passwords? Could it be more secure?

3. Why is using the same password everywhere dangerous? Share an example of what could go wrong.

# Did you know?

The most commonly used password, "123456," is cracked by hackers in less than one second! However, a 12-character password using numbers, symbols, and mixed-case letters would take approximately 34,000 years to crack using current technology.

# CHAPTER 8

## Device Defense

Photo: Adobe Photo Stock

Your devices are like your digital companions - they hold your photos, messages, games, homework, and so much more. Just like you'd protect a valuable treasure, it's important to defend your devices from various digital dangers. Let's learn how to become an expert device defender!

## Protecting Your Smartphone

Your smartphone is probably your most personal device - it goes everywhere with you and knows almost everything about you. Think about all the information it holds: your contacts, photos, messages, location data, and maybe even payment information. Protecting your smartphone is like protecting a tiny computer that happens to know all your secrets. Let's explore how to keep it safe!

### Screen Locks and Security

The first line of defense for your smartphone is a good screen lock. Think of it like the front door to your digital house - you want it to be strong and secure. While patterns and simple PINs might seem convenient, they're like using a flimsy lock. Instead, use a six-digit PIN at minimum, or better yet, combine biometric security (like fingerprint or face recognition) with a strong passcode. Remember, someone watching over your shoulder can easily memorize a pattern, but they can't steal your fingerprint!

Also, set your phone to lock automatically after a short period of not being used - 30 seconds or less is best. This is like having a door that automatically locks behind you when you leave. And speaking of automatic features, enable "Find My Phone" (for iPhone) or "Find My Device" (for Android) - these tools can help you locate your phone if it's lost, or even wipe it remotely if it's stolen.

### App Security

Your phone's app store is like a huge marketplace - while most vendors (apps) are trustworthy, some might try to sell you harmful products. Only download apps from your device's official app store (App Store for iPhone or Google Play Store for Android). Even then, read reviews and check the app's permissions before installing. If a simple flashlight app is asking for access to your contacts and location, that's a red flag!

For apps you already have, regularly review what permissions they've been granted. An app having unnecessary permissions is like giving a stranger keys to rooms in your house they don't need to access. Go through your app settings and revoke any permissions that don't make sense - does that game really need access to your microphone?

### Data Backup

Imagine losing all your photos, messages, and other important information if your phone gets lost or broken. Regular backups are like having a safety deposit box for your digital valuables. Set up automatic backups to your device's cloud service (iCloud for iPhone or Google Drive for Android) or use a computer backup. Make sure these backups are also protected with strong passwords!

## Tablet and Computer Security
While smartphones often get the most attention, tablets and computers need just as much protection. These devices often store even more sensitive information and can be more vulnerable to certain types of attacks.

## Antivirus Protection
Think of antivirus software as your device's immune system - it helps protect against various digital diseases (viruses, malware, spyware). Just as you need different medicines for different illnesses, good antivirus software protects against multiple types of threats. Make sure you have reputable antivirus software installed and keep it updated. Many operating systems come with built-in protection (like Windows Defender), but you might want additional protection, especially on computers used for downloading files or visiting lots of different websites.

## User Accounts and Admin Rights
On computers and tablets, create separate user accounts for different people - don't share one account, even with family members. Think of it like having your own room instead of sharing with siblings - it keeps your stuff separate and secure. Most importantly, don't use an administrator account for daily activities. Administrator accounts are like having master keys to the whole house - they should only be used when necessary, like installing new programs or changing important settings.

## Safe Storage
Just like you organize your physical belongings, organize your digital files in a way that makes them easy to protect. Create separate folders for different types of files (school work, personal photos, downloads) and consider encrypting sensitive information. Encryption is like putting your private files in a safe that only you have the combination to. Many devices offer built-in encryption options - use them!

## App Permission Management

Photo: Adobe Photo Stock

Understanding and managing app permissions is like being a security guard for your device - you need to know who's allowed to go where and do what. Let's master the art of controlling what apps can and can't do!

### Understanding Permissions

Different apps need different permissions to work properly. A mapping app needs your location to give directions, and a photo editing app needs access to your camera roll to edit pictures. But some apps ask for permissions they don't really need. Think of it this way: if you hired someone to clean your kitchen, would you give them access to your diary? Of course not! The same principle applies to apps. Here are some common permissions include:

- Location (GPS)
- Camera and Microphone
- Contacts
- Storage/Files
- Calendar

- Phone calls/SMS

For each permission request, ask yourself: "Does this app really need this to do its job?"

## Regular Permission Audits

Make it a habit to review app permissions regularly - think of it as doing a security check of your digital house. Go through your device's settings and look at what permissions each app has. You might be surprised to find apps with permissions they don't need or ones you no longer use that still have access to your data. Remove unnecessary permissions and uninstall apps you don't use anymore.

# Updates and Security Patches

Updates might seem annoying when they pop up, but they're actually super important for keeping your devices safe. Think of updates like vaccines for your devices - they protect against new threats and fix vulnerabilities before they can be exploited.

## Why Updates Matter

Software updates often include security patches that fix newly discovered vulnerabilities. Imagine if someone found a new way to pick locks - you'd want to upgrade your locks right away, right? That's what security patches do for your digital security. When companies discover security problems, they release updates to fix them. If you don't install these updates, your device remains vulnerable to known security risks.

## Setting Up Automatic Updates

The easiest way to stay protected is to enable automatic updates on all your devices. This is like having a security system that automatically upgrades itself whenever new threats are discovered. Set your devices to download and install updates automatically, especially security updates. The best time for updates is usually at night when you're not using your devices.

## Using Public Wi-Fi Safely

Photo: Adobe Photo Stock

Public Wi-Fi is convenient, but it can be dangerous if you're not careful. Think of public Wi-Fi like having a conversation in a crowded room - anyone might be listening! Let's learn how to use public Wi-Fi without putting your information at risk.

### Understanding the Risks

When you use public Wi-Fi, whether it's at a café, library, or mall, your data is being transmitted through a network that many other people are using. Some of these people might be trying to intercept your data. They could see what websites you're visiting, and if you're not careful, they might even be able to capture your passwords or other private information.

### Safe Public Wi-Fi Habits

Never access sensitive information (like online banking or entering credit card details) while on public Wi-Fi unless you're using a VPN (we'll talk about those next!). If you must log into accounts, use your phone's mobile data instead. Also, make sure your device doesn't automatically connect to public Wi-Fi networks - this is like blindly walking into any open door you see!

## VPN Basics for Young Users

Photo: Adobe Photo Stock

A VPN (Virtual Private Network) is like having a secret tunnel for your internet connection. Instead of your data traveling out in the open where anyone can see it, it goes through an encrypted tunnel that protects it from prying eyes.

### How VPNs Work

When you use a VPN, all your internet traffic is encrypted (scrambled) before it leaves your device. This encrypted data travels through the VPN server before going out to the internet. It's like putting your message in a locked box that only the intended recipient can open. Even if someone intercepts your data, they can't read it without the key.

### Choosing and Using a VPN

If you're interested in using a VPN, talk to your parents about choosing a reputable service. Free VPNs might seem tempting, but they often come with risks - they might collect your data or show too many ads. A good VPN should:

- Have a clear privacy policy
- Not keep logs of your activity
- Offer good connection speeds
- Have servers in multiple countries
- Provide strong encryption

## Conclusion

Defending your devices is a crucial part of staying safe in the digital world. By protecting your smartphone, securing your computer and tablet, managing app permissions, keeping software updated, using public Wi-Fi safely, and understanding VPNs, you're building a strong defense system for your digital life.

Remember, device security isn't about making your devices difficult to use - it's about making them difficult for others to misuse. With the right habits and tools, you can keep your devices both secure and convenient to use.

## Coming Up Next

Get ready to become a safe browsing expert in our next chapter, "Safe Browsing Habits"! We'll explore how to navigate the internet safely, recognize dangerous websites, protect yourself while downloading files, and use browser security features effectively. Plus, you'll learn some cool tricks for keeping your browsing private and secure. Stay tuned - your journey to becoming a digital safety expert continues!

# Your Experience With Your Device Defense

1. When was the last time you updated your devices? What stops you from updating immediately?

2. How do you protect your phone when using public Wi-Fi? What could happen if you don't?

3. What permissions have you given to your apps? Go check now - any surprises?

# Did you know?

Your smartphone has more computing power than all of NASA's combined computing power in 1969 that put two astronauts on the moon! Yet, 40% of people never update their phone's operating system, leaving it vulnerable to attacks.

# CHAPTER 9

## Safe Browsing Habits

Photo: Adobe Photo Stock

Welcome to the world of safe web browsing! The internet is like a vast city with millions of websites to explore. Just as you'd want a map and some street smarts to explore a real city safely, you need digital street smarts to explore the internet. Let's learn how to navigate the web while keeping yourself and your information safe!

## Browser Security Settings

Your web browser (like Chrome, Safari, Firefox, or Edge) is your vehicle for exploring the internet, and just like a car needs good safety features to keep you protected on the road, your browser needs proper security settings to keep you safe online. Most browsers come with built-in security features, but you need to make sure they're turned on and set up correctly.

## Privacy Settings

Think of your browser's privacy settings as your digital sunglasses and disguise. They help control what websites can see about you and what information they can collect. Start by opening your browser's settings and looking for the Privacy or Security section. Here's what you should adjust:

First, turn on "Do Not Track" requests. While not all websites honor these requests, it's like putting up a "No Photos Please" sign - it tells websites you don't want them tracking your activities. Next, disable third-party cookies. Cookies are like little digital notes that websites leave on your computer to remember things about you. While some cookies are helpful (like remembering your language preferences), third-party cookies are often used to track you across different websites.

Consider using your browser's enhanced tracking protection if available. Firefox calls this "Enhanced Tracking Protection," while Safari has "Intelligent Tracking Prevention." These features are like having a bodyguard who stops websites from following you around the internet.

## Security Features

Your browser's security features are like your digital armor. They help protect you from harmful websites and dangerous downloads. Enable "Safe Browsing" or "SmartScreen" (depending on your browser) - these features check websites against a list of known dangerous sites and warn you before you visit them.

Make sure your browser is set to block pop-ups by default. Pop-ups are like strangers jumping out at you while you're walking - most are just annoying, but some can be dangerous. Also, enable the setting to warn you before visiting suspected dangerous websites. This is like having a friend who knows which neighborhoods to avoid!

# Safe Search Techniques

Photo: Adobe Photo Stock

Searching the internet is like going on a treasure hunt - you're looking for specific information in a sea of websites. But just as you wouldn't want to find fool's gold instead of real treasure, you need to know how to search safely and find reliable information.

## Using Safe Search Engines

Start with trusted search engines like Google, Bing, or DuckDuckGo. Each has its own special features, but they all offer ways to search safely. Enable "Safe Search" in your search engine settings - this helps filter out inappropriate content, like having a special pair of glasses that only shows you kid-friendly results.

Remember that search engines are like tour guides - they can take you to different places on the internet, but they can't guarantee every place is safe. Even with Safe Search on, you need to think carefully about which search results you click.

## Evaluating Search Results

Before clicking on any search result, look at the URL (web address) carefully.

Is it from a website you recognize? Does the URL match what you expect it to be? For example, if you're looking for information about pandas from National Geographic, the URL should start with "nationalgeographic.com," not something like "totally-real-panda-facts.com."

Pay attention to the short description under each search result. Does it match what you're looking for? Be especially careful with results marked as "Ad" or "Sponsored" - these are like billboards that companies have paid for, and they might not be the most reliable sources of information.

## Download Safety

Downloading files from the internet is like accepting packages from strangers - you need to be very careful about what you're receiving and who you're receiving it from. Let's learn how to download safely!

### Safe Download Sources

Only download files from websites you trust completely. Official app stores, well-known software companies, and established educational websites are usually safe sources. Think of these like official stores in a mall - they have a reputation to protect and security measures in place.

Be especially careful with files that end in .exe, .dmg, .zip, or .app - these are program files that can run on your computer and potentially cause harm if they're from untrustworthy sources. It's like being careful about accepting wrapped packages from strangers - you can't see what's inside until it's too late!

### Checking Downloads

Before opening any downloaded file, scan it with your antivirus software. This is like having a security guard check packages for dangerous items before you open them. Many browsers and operating systems do this automatically, but it's good to double-check.

Watch out for fake download buttons! Some websites have multiple buttons that say "Download" or "Start Download," but only one is real - the others might lead to unwanted programs or harmful files. Take your time to find the correct download link, usually near the actual content you want to download.

## Ad Blockers and Security Extensions

Photo: Adobe Photo Stock

Browser extensions are like helpful tools you can add to your browser to make it safer and more useful. Ad blockers and security extensions are particularly important for safe browsing - they're like having a personal security team that helps protect you while you explore the internet.

### Understanding Ad Blockers

Ad blockers do more than just hide annoying advertisements - they can also protect you from dangerous ads that might try to install malware or trick you into clicking on harmful links. Think of an ad blocker like a shield that blocks both annoying and dangerous content from reaching you.

Popular ad blockers like uBlock Origin or AdBlock Plus can be installed from your browser's extension store. Once installed, they work automatically to block most ads. However, remember that some websites rely on advertising to provide free content, so you might want to support your favorite sites by allowing non-intrusive ads.

### Security Extensions

Security extensions add extra layers of protection to your browsing. Here are some essential ones to consider:

HTTPS Everywhere ensures you connect to the secure version of websites whenever possible. It's like making sure you're always walking on the safe side of the street. Web of Trust (WoT) shows you which websites other users trust or don't trust - it's like having a crowd of friendly internet users warning you about dangerous sites.

Password managers, which we discussed in the previous chapter, often come with browser extensions that make it easier to use strong, unique passwords on every website. Think of this like having a secure key chain that automatically picks the right key for each door you need to open.

## Recognizing Fake Websites

Photo: Adobe Photo Stock

Fake websites are like wolves in sheep's clothing - they try to look like legitimate sites to trick you into sharing personal information or downloading harmful files. Learning to spot these imposters is a crucial skill for safe browsing.

## URL Detective Work

Become a URL detective! The web address can tell you a lot about whether a website is real or fake. Look carefully at the domain name (the main part of the website address). Scammers often use tricks like:

- Misspellings (amazon.com instead of amazon.com)
- Added words (facebook-login-secure.com instead of facebook.com)
- Different endings (.net or .org instead of .com)

Think of it like checking the address of a store - if you're going to your local bank but the address is completely different from what you expected, that's a big red flag!

## Signs of Fake Websites

Fake websites often have tell-tale signs that can help you spot them:

Poor Design and Grammar: Legitimate companies spend time and money making their websites look professional. If you see lots of spelling mistakes, weird fonts, or a design that looks outdated or unprofessional, be suspicious. It's like walking into a store that claims to sell expensive products but looks like it was set up in a hurry.

Pressure Tactics: Fake websites often try to create urgency with messages like "Act now!" or "Only 1 minute left!" They want you to act quickly before you notice something's wrong. It's like someone trying to rush you into buying something without giving you time to think about it.

Unusual Payment Methods: Be very suspicious if a website only accepts unusual payment methods like wire transfers or gift cards. Legitimate websites usually accept credit cards and well-known payment services like PayPal.

## Conclusion

Safe browsing habits are your passport to enjoying all the amazing things the internet has to offer while staying protected from its dangers. By understanding and using browser security settings, practicing safe search techniques, being careful with downloads, using helpful extensions, and learning to spot fake websites, you're building the skills you need to navigate the digital world safely.

Remember, safe browsing isn't about being afraid of the internet - it's about being smart and prepared. Just like you can have fun exploring a city while staying aware of your surroundings, you can enjoy exploring the internet while staying safe from digital dangers.

## Coming Up Next

Get ready to become a digital communication expert in our next chapter, "Digital Communication Safety"! We'll explore how to keep your emails, messages, and video chats secure and private. You'll learn about encryption, safe file sharing, and how to handle unknown contacts. Plus, we'll share some cool tips for keeping your conversations private while still enjoying all the benefits of digital communication. Stay tuned - your journey to becoming a digital safety expert continues!

# Your Thought on Safe Browsing Habits

1. How can you tell if a website is safe to use? What clues do you look for?

2. Share a time when you almost fell for a scam website. What warned you?

3. What browser extensions do you use to stay safe? How do they help?

# Did you know?

The average person spends 6 months of their lifetime waiting for websites to load! And in that time, your device connects to approximately 100 different servers for a single web page to load completely.

# CHAPTER 10

## Digital Communication Safety

Photo: Adobe Photo Stock

In today's world, connecting with others through digital communication is integral to our everyday lives. Whether chatting with friends face-to-face, enjoying virtual hangouts, or exchanging messages across different platforms, these interactions have transformed the way we engage with one another. But just as you need to be careful about who you talk to and what you share in the real world, you need to be smart about how you communicate online. Let's learn how to keep all your digital conversations safe and secure!

## Email Security

Photo: Adobe Photo Stock

Email might seem old-school compared to social media and messaging apps, but it's still super important - especially for school, family communication, and eventually work. Think of email like sending letters through a digital post office. Just as you wouldn't want strangers reading your personal letters or sending fake mail in your name, you need to protect your email from various threats.

### Creating a Secure Email Account

Your email address is like your digital home address - it needs to be appropriate and secure. When creating an email address, use something professional that doesn't reveal too much personal information. Create a strong, unique password for your email account - remember, if someone hacks your email, they could access many of your other accounts through password reset links!

For example, "jane.smith2024@email.com" is better than "janeloves cats11@email.com" or "jane2010nyc@email.com" (which reveals your location or birth year).

## Spotting Email Scams

Email scams are like digital tricksters trying to fool you into giving away your secrets or clicking on dangerous links. One common type is phishing emails - these try to look like they're from legitimate companies or people you trust. Be extra careful with emails that:

- Claim there's an urgent problem with your account
- Say you've won something amazing (that you never entered to win)
- Ask you to verify your password or personal information
- Include attachments you weren't expecting
- Have lots of spelling mistakes or look unprofessional

**Real-World Example:** Sarah got an email that looked like it was from her school, saying she needed to log in immediately to see an important message about her grades. The email had a link, but when she looked carefully, she noticed the web address wasn't quite right - it was "yoursch00l.com" instead of her school's real website. She showed the email to her teacher, who confirmed it was a scam.

## Email Safety Best Practices

Think of your email inbox like your home's front door - you need to be careful about what (and who) you let in. Never open attachments from people you don't know - they could contain viruses or other harmful programs. Be careful about clicking links in emails, even if they seem to be from people you know. If something seems suspicious, contact the sender through another method (like calling or texting them) to verify they really sent the email.

## Messaging App Safety

Photo: Adobe Photo Stock

Messaging apps are probably your main way of staying in touch with friends. Whether you're using WhatsApp, iMessage, Discord, or other apps, it's important to understand how to use them safely. Think of these apps like having different types of conversations - some are private like whispering to a best friend, while others are more public like talking in the school cafeteria.

### Choosing Secure Messaging Apps

Not all messaging apps are equally secure. Look for apps that offer end-to-end encryption - this means your messages are scrambled so only you and the person you're sending them to can read them. It's like having a secret code that only you and your friend know! Popular secure messaging apps include Signal, WhatsApp, and iMessage. Remember, though, that even with secure apps, screenshots can still be taken and shared.

### Group Chat Safety

Group chats can be super fun but also risky if you're not careful. Before joining a group chat, know who's in it and who can add new members. Be careful about sharing personal information in group chats - remember that you might not know everyone in the group personally. Also, be aware that leaving a group chat doesn't automatically delete your previous messages - think carefully about what you share!

## Message Privacy Settings

Take time to review and adjust these settings for each app you use. Think of it like choosing what you want to share with different groups of friends in real life. Most messaging apps let you control things like:

- Who can see when you're online
- Who can see your profile photo
- Who can see your status or stories
- Who can add you to groups

## Video Chat Safety

Photo: Adobe Photo Stock

Video chatting has become a huge part of how we connect with friends and family, especially when we can't meet in person. But video chats can also expose more of your life than you might realize - your room, your family members in the background, or personal items visible behind you. Let's learn how to video chat safely!

## Setting Up Safe Video Chats

Before starting any video chat, think about your environment. What can others see in your background? Are there any personal items, photos, or documents visible? Consider using virtual backgrounds or setting up in front of a plain wall. Think of it like choosing what part of your home to show visitors - you probably wouldn't let strangers walk through your whole house!

## Video Chat Privacy Settings

Learn how to use features like waiting rooms, meeting passwords, and participant controls. These are like having a security guard who checks people before letting them into your video chat. Never share video chat links or passwords publicly - send them directly to the people who need them.

## Video Chat Etiquette and Safety

Remember that anything that happens in a video chat could be recorded or screenshot, even if you can't tell it's happening. Be mindful of what you say and do, just as you would in person. If you're ever uncomfortable in a video chat, it's okay to turn off your camera or leave the meeting. Trust your instincts!

## Dealing with Unknown Contacts

Getting messages or contact requests from strangers is like having someone you don't know try to start a conversation on the street - you need to be careful about how you respond (or whether to respond at all).

## Identifying Safe Contacts

Just because someone claims to know you or have mutual friends doesn't mean they're safe to talk to. Be especially careful of people who:

- Say they know you but can't explain exactly how
- Claim to be someone famous or important
- Try to keep your conversation secret from others
- Ask lots of personal questions

- Try to move the conversation to private messages quickly

## Handling Unknown Contact Requests

When you get a contact request from unknown person, follow these steps:

- Check if you have any real-life connections (like being in the same school or club)
- Look at their profile for signs it might be fake (like being brand new or having very little information)
- If you're unsure, ask a parent or trusted adult for advice
- Remember it's okay to ignore or block requests from people you don't know

## Sharing Files Safely

Sharing files online is like passing notes in class - you want to make sure they get to the right person and nobody else can read them. Whether you're sharing homework assignments, photos, or other files, you need to know how to do it safely.

## Safe File Sharing Methods

Avoid sharing files through public posts or unsecured websites. Use secure methods to share files:

- Cloud storage services (like Google Drive or Dropbox) with proper sharing settings
- Direct messaging in secure apps
- Email attachments (but be careful with large or sensitive files)

## Checking Files Before Sharing

Think of it like double-checking a letter before sealing the envelope - once you send it, you can't take it back! Before sharing any file, check:

- Is there any personal information in the file or the file name?
- Could the file contain anything inappropriate or embarrassing?
- Are you sure about who will have access to the file?
- Do you have permission to share this file?

## Receiving Shared Files

Be careful about files others share with you particularly from unknown sources, as these files put you at cybersecurity risks:

- Don't open files from people you don't know
- Be cautious about files you weren't expecting, even from friends
- Scan files for viruses before opening them
- Never open files that end in .exe unless you're absolutely sure they're safe

## Conclusion

Digital communication is amazing - it lets us stay connected with friends and family, work on projects together, and share experiences even when we're far apart. But just like in-person communication, we need to be smart about how we do it. By using secure apps, being careful about what we share, and knowing how to handle unknown contacts, we can enjoy all the benefits of digital communication while staying safe.

Remember, being safe online doesn't mean you can't have fun or be yourself - it just means being thoughtful about how you communicate and who you communicate with. Think of these safety practices like the rules of any game — to make sure everyone can play and have fun without getting hurt.

## Coming Up Next

Get ready to sharpen your detective skills in our next chapter, "Being a Digital Detective"! We'll explore how to spot fake news, verify information online, and understand digital manipulation. You'll learn cool techniques for fact-checking, recognizing edited photos and videos, and finding reliable sources for information. Plus, we'll share some amazing tools that can help you become a master digital truth-seeker. Stay tuned - your journey to becoming a digital safety expert continues!

# Your Thought on Digital Communication Safety

1. How do you verify that someone online is who they claim to be?

2. What's your strategy for handling messages from unknown senders?

3. When sharing files online, what precautions do you take?

# Did you know?

Every email you send travels through an average of 15 different computers before reaching its destination! During this journey, an unencrypted email can be read at any of these points - like sending a postcard through the mail.

# CHAPTER 10

## Being a Digital Detective

Photo: Adobe Photo Stock

In today's world, information is everywhere - but not all of it is true. Just like a real detective needs to gather clues and solve mysteries, you need skills to figure out what's real and what's fake online. Get ready to learn some awesome detective techniques that will help you become an expert at spotting truth from fiction in the digital world!

## Fact-Checking Skills

Photo: Adobe Photo Stock

Think of fact-checking like being a truth detective - you're gathering evidence to determine if something is true or false. Just like detectives don't believe everything they hear and look for proof instead, you need to develop the habit of questioning information you find online and knowing how to verify it.

## Three-Step Fact Check

When you come across information online, use this three-step process to check if it's true:

- First, ask yourself if it sounds believable. Does it match what you already know about the topic? If someone tells you that scientists have discovered unicorns, your first reaction should be skepticism - this doesn't match what we know about real animals. But don't stop there - sometimes true things can sound unbelievable, and false things can sound very convincing!

- Next, check the source. Who is sharing this information? Is it coming from a reliable source like a well-known news organization, educational institution, or expert in the field? Or is it from someone's personal blog or social media post? Think of sources like witnesses in a detective case - some are more reliable than others.

- Finally, cross-reference the information. Can you find the same information from other reliable sources? If a story is true, it usually appears on multiple trustworthy news sites or educational platforms. If you can only find the information on one website or social media post, that's a red flag.

## Using Fact-Checking Websites

Several websites specialize in fact-checking popular claims and news stories. Think of these sites like detective agencies that investigate viral stories and popular claims. Some reliable fact-checking websites include:

- Snopes.com - Great for checking viral stories and urban legends
- FactCheck.org - Focuses on political claims and science facts
- PolitiFact - Rates the accuracy of statements by public figures
- Reuters Fact Check - Investigates viral claims and photos

When using these sites, remember they're tools to help you think critically, not absolute authorities. Even fact-checkers can sometimes make mistakes or miss important context.

## Spotting Fake News and Scams

Fake news and scams are like master disguise artists - they try to look real to trick people into believing or sharing them. Learning to spot them is a crucial skill in today's digital world.

## Anatomy of Fake News

Fake news often has telltale signs that can help you identify it. First, check the emotional reaction - fake news often tries to make you feel very angry, scared, or excited. Real news typically aims to inform rather than provoke strong emotions. It's like when someone tries too hard to convince you of something - that extra push often means they're not telling the truth.

Look at the writing style and presentation. Professional news organizations have editors who check for spelling and grammar mistakes. If you see lots of errors, ALL CAPS, or excessive exclamation points (!!!!), these are red flags. Also, check the dates - sometimes old news stories are recirculated as if they're new, like trying to sell yesterday's newspaper as today's news.

## Common Scam Patterns

Online scams often follow predictable patterns, just like criminals often have signature methods. Be especially careful of:

- Offers that seem too good to be true
- Messages creating artificial urgency ("Act now!")
- Requests for personal information or money
- Stories that play on your emotions or fears
- Promises of exclusive or secret information

**Real-world example:** Jamie saw a social media post about a popular game giving away free in-game currency. The post looked official and had thousands of likes. But when Jamie checked the game's official website and social media accounts, there was no mention of this giveaway. This was a classic scam trying to steal account information from players.

## Understanding Digital Manipulation

Photo: Adobe Photo Stock

Digital manipulation is like having a magic wand that can change how things look or sound online. While this can be fun for art and entertainment, it's also used to deceive people. Learning to spot manipulated content is an important detective skill.

## Photo and Video Manipulation

Today's technology makes it easy to edit photos and videos to show things that never happened. Think of it like a digital special effects movie - what you see might look real but could be completely created or altered. Some signs of manipulation include:

Odd Lighting or Shadows: If the lighting on different parts of an image doesn't match, or if shadows fall in impossible directions, the image might be edited. It's like noticing that everyone in a group photo has their shadow pointing in a different direction - that's not how light works!

Warped Backgrounds: When people edit images, they sometimes accidentally distort the background. Look for bent lines that should be straight, or patterns that don't flow naturally. This is like noticing that the wallpaper in a room suddenly bends around a person - that's not normal!

## Deep Fakes and AI-Generated Content

Deep fakes are like digital actors that can make it look like real people are saying or doing things they never actually did. They're created using artificial intelligence, and they're getting more convincing every day. Some ways to spot deep fakes:

- Watch for unnatural movement, especially around mouth and eyes
- Listen for changes in voice tone or unusual speech patterns
- Look for inconsistencies in lighting and skin tone
- Check if the content matches known facts about the person

## Verifying Online Information

Being able to verify information is like having a truth compass - it helps you navigate through the sea of online content and find what's reliable. Let's learn some techniques for verifying different types of online information.

## Reverse Image Search

Reverse image search is like being able to trace a picture back to its source. If you see a dramatic photo online, you can use tools like Google Images,

TinEye, or Yandex to find where the image originally came from. This can help you:

- Discover if an image has been edited
- Find out when the image was first published
- See if the image is being used out of context
- Verify if the story matching the image is true

For example, sometimes people share photos of one event and claim they're from another. A reverse image search can show you when and where the photo was really taken.

## Cross-Referencing Information

Think of cross-referencing like getting multiple witnesses to verify a story. When you find interesting information online:

- Check if other reliable sources are reporting the same thing
- Look for original sources and research papers
- Compare different versions of the story
- Check if experts in the field agree with the information

## Evaluating Website Credibility

Not all websites are equally trustworthy. Think of websites like different types of stores - some are well-established and reliable, while others might be temporary or dishonest. Check:

- Domain names (.edu, .gov are usually more reliable)
- About pages and contact information
- Professional design and functionality
- Regular updates and maintenance
- Citations and references to sources

## Safe Research Techniques

When you're doing research online, whether for school projects or personal interest, you need to be both effective and safe. Let's explore how to find the information you need while protecting yourself.

## Using Safe Search Engines

Start with search engines designed for students and educational purposes. These often filter out inappropriate content and prioritize educational sources. Some good options include:

- Sweet Search (designed for students)
- Kids.gov (for government and historical information)
- KidzSearch (filtered search engine for young users)
- Google Scholar (for academic sources)

## Evaluating Sources

When researching, think of sources like different types of experts. Just as you'd trust a doctor more than a random person for medical advice, some sources are more reliable than others for different topics. Consider:

- Who wrote the information?
- What are their qualifications?
- When was it written or updated?
- Where is it published?
- Why was it written?
- How does it compare to other sources?

## Safe Note-Taking

Notes taking are common part of online search, so keep in mind when taking notes from online sources:

- Always record where you found the information
- Use quotation marks for direct quotes
- Summarize information in your own words
- Keep track of URLs and access dates
- Save important pages as PDFs or screenshots in case they change

## Conclusion

Being a digital detective isn't just about spotting what's fake - it's about developing critical thinking skills that will help you throughout your life. By learning to fact-check, spot manipulation, verify information, and research safely, you're building important skills for the digital age.

Remember, good detectives don't jump to conclusions. They gather evidence, check facts, and think critically about what they find. Use these skills to help yourself and others navigate the online world more safely and intelligently.

## Coming Up Next

Get ready to become a responsible digital citizen in our next chapter, "Becoming a Digital Citizen"! We'll explore how to use your new detective skills to make the internet a better place for everyone. You'll learn about digital ethics, building a positive online reputation, and ways to help others stay safe online. Plus, we'll share some exciting ideas for using your digital powers for good! Stay tuned - your journey to becoming a digital safety expert is almost complete!

# Your Strategy Being a Digital Detective

4. How do you fact-check information you find online? Share your process.

5. Have you ever spotted fake news? How did you know it was fake?

6. What tools do you use to verify if images or videos have been manipulated?

# Did you know?

Over 90% of online images have been edited or manipulated in some way! But here's the shocking part: studies show that humans can only detect fake images about 60% of the time, making us worse at spotting fakes than random guessing.

CHAPTER 12

# Becoming a Digital Citizen

Photo: Adobe Photo Stock

Y ou must be exciting to become a digital citizen of our hyperly connected world! Just like being a good citizen in your community means following rules, helping others, and making your neighborhood a better place, being a good digital citizen means contributing positively to the online world. Let's explore how you can become an awesome

112

digital citizen who makes the internet better for everyone!

## Digital Ethics and Responsibility

Digital ethics is like having a moral compass for the online world. It helps you navigate tricky situations and make good choices about how you behave online. Just as you have responsibilities in the real world (like being kind to others and respecting property), you have important responsibilities in the digital world too.

## Understanding Digital Ethics

Think of digital ethics as the "golden rules" of the internet. These principles help guide our online behavior and decisions. For example, just because you can copy and paste someone else's work doesn't mean you should - that's plagiarism, and it's both wrong and often illegal. Similarly, just because you can post something embarrassing about someone doesn't mean it's right to do so. Digital ethics involves thinking about how your online actions affect others and making choices that respect everyone's rights and feelings.

Consider this situation: You find a funny photo of your friend making a silly face. You could share it instantly with everyone you know, but digital ethics would have you stop and think: Would sharing this hurt your friend's feelings? Did they give permission to share the photo? How would you feel if someone shared an embarrassing photo of you? These kinds of thoughtful considerations are at the heart of digital ethics.

## Digital Responsibilities

Being online comes with real responsibilities. Think of these as your digital duties - the things you should do to be a good member of the online community. These include:

**Protecting Intellectual Property:** Just as you wouldn't steal something from a store, you shouldn't steal digital content. This means not copying other people's work without permission, giving credit when you use someone else's ideas, and respecting copyright laws. For example, if you're making a video for your social media, you can't just use any music you like - you need to use royalty-free music or get permission from the creator.

**Being Truthful:** In the digital world, it's easy to pretend to be someone else or spread information without checking if it's true. But being a good digital citizen means being honest about who you are (while still protecting your privacy) and helping to stop the spread of false information. If you're not sure something is true, take the time to verify it before sharing.

## Building a Positive Online Reputation

Your online reputation is like a digital shadow that follows you everywhere - and unlike real shadows, this one can last forever! Everything you post, comment, or share becomes part of your digital footprint, which can affect your future opportunities for school, work, and relationships.

## Creating a Positive Digital Presence

Building a positive online presence is like planting a garden - it takes time, care, and good choices to grow something beautiful. Start by thinking about how you want others to see you online. Are you passionate about art? Share your creations and support other artists. Love science? Share interesting facts and engage in thoughtful discussions about scientific discoveries. Whatever your interests, focus on contributing positive, constructive content to the online world.

**Real World Example:** Maria is a 14-year-old who loves baking. Instead of just posting selfies, she created a blog where she shares her favorite recipes, baking tips, and photos of both her successes and failures. Her positive, honest approach has not only built her a good reputation but also helped create a supportive community of young bakers.

## Managing Your Digital Identity

Think of your digital identity like a portfolio that showcases the best of who you are. Before posting anything, ask yourself:

- Would I be proud to show this to my grandparents?
- Could this post help or inspire others?
- Would I want future teachers or employers to see this?
- Does this represent who I really am and want to be?

Remember, it's not about being perfect - it's about being authentic and thoughtful about what you share online.

## Supporting Others Online

The internet can be a powerful tool for supporting and uplifting others. Think of it like having a superpower - you can use your online presence to help people feel better, learn new things, and overcome challenges.

## Creating Supportive Communities

Just as you might help create a welcoming environment in your school or neighborhood, you can help create positive online spaces. This might mean:

Starting a study group chat where classmates can help each other with homework: Jake noticed many of his classmates struggling with math, so he created a Discord server where students could share problems, explain solutions, and encourage each other. The group helped everyone improve their grades and created new friendships.

Creating an online club for shared interests: Sarah loved drawing anime characters but didn't know anyone at school who shared her interest. She started an online art club where young artists could share their work, give constructive feedback, and support each other's creativity.

## Being a Digital Mentor

Photo: Adobe Photo Stock

As you develop your digital skills, you can help others learn to navigate the online world safely. Maybe you could:

- Help younger siblings understand online safety
- Show grandparents how to use video chat safely
- Guide friends in protecting their privacy online
- Share digital literacy tips with your community

## Reporting Problems

Photo: Adobe Photo Stock

When you see problems online, being a good digital citizen means taking appropriate action. It's like being part of a neighborhood watch program - you help keep the community safe by reporting things that aren't right.

### When and How to Report

Understanding when and how to report problems is crucial. Some situations that should be reported include:

**Cyberbullying:** If you see someone being harassed or bullied online, don't just scroll past. Most platforms have simple ways to report bullying behavior. For example, Tom noticed someone leaving mean comments on his friend's posts. Instead of arguing with the bully, he used the platform's reporting tool and encouraged his friend to block the harasser.

**Harmful Content:** This includes things like hate speech, explicit content, or dangerous misinformation. Katie found a post spreading false information about a fake cure for a serious illness. She reported the post and shared correct information from reliable medical sources.

## Using Reporting Tools Effectively

Most social media platforms and websites have built-in reporting tools. Learn how to use these effectively:

- Be specific about what you're reporting
- Include screenshots or examples when possible
- Follow up if the problem continues
- Know when to involve trusted adults

## Being an Upstander, Not a Bystander

An upstander is someone who takes action when they see something wrong, while a bystander just watches. In the digital world, being an upstander is crucial for creating a better online environment for everyone.

## Recognizing Opportunities to Help

Being an upstander means being alert to situations where you can make a positive difference. For example:

When you see someone being excluded: Alex noticed that classmates were ignoring a new student in the class group chat. Instead of staying quiet, he made an effort to include the new student in discussions and encouraged others to do the same.

When misinformation is spreading: Maya saw friends sharing a scary but false rumor about a local event. Instead of scrolling past, she politely shared accurate information from reliable sources and explained why spreading rumors can be harmful.

## Taking Safe and Effective Action

Being an upstander doesn't mean putting yourself at risk. There are many ways to help:

- Support the person being targeted
- Get help from trusted adults
- Use reporting tools
- Share positive and accurate information
- Stand together with others against harmful behavior

Sometimes the most effective action is simply showing kindness and support to someone who's being treated unfairly online.

## Conclusion

Being a digital citizen isn't just about using technology - it's about making the online world a better place through your actions and choices. By understanding digital ethics, building a positive reputation, supporting others, reporting problems, and being an upstander, you become part of the solution to online challenges.

Remember, every positive action you take online, no matter how small, helps create a better digital world for everyone. Your choices and actions matter, and you have the power to influence others and make real positive changes in the digital world.

## Coming Up Next

Get ready for action in our next chapter, "When Things Go Wrong"! We'll explore what to do in different digital emergency situations, from handling cyberbullying to recovering from hacks. You'll learn practical steps to take when facing online problems and know exactly when and how to get help from others. Plus, we'll share some real stories of young people who successfully handled digital challenges. Stay tuned - your journey to becoming a digital safety expert is getting even more exciting!

# Your Understanding of a Good Digital Citizen

1. What does being a good digital citizen mean to you?

2. Share a time when you stood up against cyberbullying. What happened?

3. How do you try to make the internet a better place for others?

# Did you know?

Your first social media post might still exist even if you deleted it! The Library of Congress has been archiving every single public tweet since 2006, and numerous other organizations keep archives of deleted social media posts.

# CHAPTER 13

## When Things Go Wrong

Photo: Adobe Photo Stock

S ometimes, despite our best efforts to stay safe online, things can go wrong. Just like you need to know what to do in case of a fire or other emergency, it's important to know how to handle digital emergencies. Don't worry - we'll walk through exactly what to do in different situations and help you get back on track!

## Signs You've Been Hacked

Photo: Adobe Photo Stock

Just like your body shows symptoms when you're getting sick, your devices and accounts show signs when they've been hacked. Learning to recognize these signs early can help you stop the problem before it gets worse. Let's explore the warning signs that might indicate you've been hacked.

### Strange Account Behavior

One of the first signs that something's wrong might be unexpected changes in your accounts. Think of it like coming home to find your room rearranged - you know something's not right because things aren't where you left them. Watch for signs like:

Your password stops working even though you know you're typing it correctly - this could mean someone changed it. Maybe you notice posts or messages you didn't create appearing on your social media accounts. Friends might tell you they're getting strange messages from you that you never sent. For example, Emma knew something was wrong when her friends started asking about weird game links she supposedly sent them through Instagram - links she'd never actually shared.

## Device Warning Signs

Your devices might also show signs of being hacked. Imagine your phone or computer catching a digital cold - it might start acting strangely. Look out for:

Your device suddenly becoming very slow or hot, like it's working extra hard even when you're not doing much. New apps or programs appearing that you didn't install. Your browser homepage changing without your permission, or strange pop-ups appearing even when you're not on the internet. These could all be signs that someone has gained unauthorized access to your device.

## What to Do If You're Being Cyberbullied

Photo: Adobe Photo Stock

Cyberbullying is like regular bullying, but it can follow you home through your devices. It's never okay, and you don't have to face it alone. Let's talk about what you can do if someone is bullying you online.

## Immediate Steps to Take

The moment you realize you're being cyberbullied, take these important first steps such as not responding to the bully. It's like adding fuel to a fire -

responding often makes things worse. Instead, take screenshots of the bullying messages or posts. These are your evidence, like taking pictures after a car accident - they prove what happened. Then, block the person who's bullying you on all platforms. You don't have to keep channels open for people who are hurting you.

## Building Your Support System

You might feel embarrassed or scared to tell someone about cyberbullying, but getting help is really important. Think of it like having a team on your side and start by telling a trusted adult - a parent, teacher, school counselor, or another adult you trust. They can help you figure out what to do next and support you emotionally. Keep a record of what's happening - write down dates, times, and what occurred. This can help adults understand the situation better and take action to help you.

## Taking Care of Yourself

Being cyberbullied can make you feel awful, but there are things you can do to feel better: such as take breaks from social media or devices if you need to - it's like stepping away from a noisy room to find some peace. Spend time with friends who make you feel good about yourself. Do activities you enjoy offline. Remember that the bullying is not your fault, and you don't deserve to be treated this way.

## Dealing with Online Harassment

Online harassment can be scarier than cyberbullying because it might come from strangers and feel more threatening. But there are specific steps you can take to protect yourself and stop the harassment.

## Recognizing Online Harassment

Online harassment can take many forms, and it's important to recognize when normal online behavior crosses the line into harassment. If someone keeps contacting you after you've asked them to stop, that's harassment. If they're making threats, sharing private information about you (doxing), or trying to embarrass you publicly, these are serious forms of harassment. For example, Jack started getting threatening messages from someone claiming to know where he lived after he won an online game. This wasn't just bad sportsmanship - it was harassment.

## Safety Steps

When dealing with online harassment, your safety should be your top priority is to document everything - save screenshots, emails, or messages that show the harassment. Never share personal information with someone who's harassing you, even if they threaten you. Use all available privacy settings to block the harasser and protect your accounts. If the harassment includes threats of violence or sharing private images, this needs to be reported to both the platform and possibly the police.

## Reporting Cybercrime

Cybercrime is any crime that happens online or using digital devices. Just like you'd report a stolen bike to the police, there are ways to report digital crimes to the proper authorities.

## Understanding of Cybercrimes

Understanding what counts as cybercrime can help you know when to report it. Identity theft, online scams, hacking, and serious harassment are all types of cybercrime. If someone is trying to trick you into sending money or personal information, that's probably a crime. If they're threatening you or sharing private images without permission, that's likely a crime too. For example, Sarah received an email claiming to be from her bank, asking for her password. She recognized this as a potential crime (phishing) and reported it.

## How to Report

Different types of cybercrime might need to be reported to different places. Start by reporting the incident to the platform where it happened (like the social media site or gaming platform). Many countries have special cybercrime reporting websites or hotlines - ask an adult to help you find the right one. Your school might also have specific procedures for reporting digital incidents that happen between students.

## Getting Help from Adults

Sometimes kids worry that adults won't understand digital problems or might make things worse by overreacting. But adults can be your best allies in dealing with online problems - you just need to know how to talk to them effectively.

## Choosing the Right Adult

Think carefully about which adult to talk to and look for someone who listens without judging and takes your concerns seriously. This might be a parent, teacher, school counselor, coach, or another trusted adult. They don't need to be a tech expert - they just need to be willing to help you figure things out. Sometimes it helps to talk to more than one adult, as different people might have different helpful perspectives or resources.

## How to Explain the Problem

When telling an adult about a digital problem, be clear and specific. Show them exactly what happened using screenshots or by walking them through the situation step by step. Explain what you've already tried to do about the problem. Be honest about everything - even if you made some mistakes, adults will be better able to help if they know the whole story.

## Recovery Steps After an Incident

Photo: Adobe Photo Stock

After dealing with any kind of digital problem, it's important to take steps to recover and prevent future incidents. Think of it like cleaning up and reinforcing your house after a storm.

## Digital Recovery

Start by securing all your accounts and devices. Change passwords on all your accounts, even ones you don't think were affected. Review and update your privacy settings. Remove any apps or programs you don't recognize or trust. Back up your important files if you haven't already. Think of this as your digital clean-up operation.

## Emotional Recovery

Digital incidents can be really upsetting, and it's important to take care of your emotional health too. Give yourself time to feel better - just like recovering from a physical injury, emotional recovery takes time. Talk about your feelings with people you trust. Learn from what happened but try not to let it make you too scared to use the internet - instead, use it as motivation to be more secure in the future.

## Prevention Steps

Use what you've learned to better protect yourself going forward. Set up better security measures like two-factor authentication on your accounts. Create a plan for what you'll do if something similar happens again. Share what you've learned with friends so they can protect themselves too. Remember, experiencing a digital problem doesn't make you stupid or naive - even experts sometimes have security issues. What matters is how you recover and what you learn from it.

## Conclusion

When things go wrong online, it's important to remember that you're not alone and there are always steps you can take to make things better. By knowing the signs of problems, understanding how to get help, and taking proper recovery steps, you can handle digital emergencies effectively and come out stronger.

Remember, experiencing a digital problem doesn't mean you did anything wrong - but how you handle it can make a big difference in the outcome. Stay calm, follow the steps we've discussed, and don't be afraid to ask for help when you need it.

## Coming Up Next

Get ready to build your personal safety plan in our next chapter, "Creating Your Safety Plan"! We'll help you create a customized plan that fits your digital life, including checklists for regular security checks, emergency contact lists, and family discussion guides. You'll learn how to prevent problems before they happen and be prepared for any digital situation. Plus, we'll provide templates and tools to make it easy to keep track of your safety practices. Stay tuned - you're about to become a master of digital safety planning!

# Your Thought on Cyber Crisis Strategy

1. What would you do first if your account was hacked? Who would you tell?

2. How would you help a friend who's being cyberbullied?

3. What's your emergency plan for digital problems? Write it down now!

# Did you know?

Cybercrime happens faster than you think! A hacker attacks someone on the internet every 39 seconds, and new devices connected to the internet are usually attacked within 5 minutes of going online.

# CHAPTER 14

## Creating Your Safety Plan

Photo: Adobe Photo Stock

Welcome to the final chapter of your journey to becoming a digital safety expert! Just like having a fire escape plan for your home or knowing what to do in case of an emergency at school, having a digital safety plan is super important. Let's create your personal plan to stay safe online!

## Personal Security Checklist

Think of your personal security checklist as your daily digital hygiene routine - just like you brush your teeth and wash your hands to stay healthy, you need regular digital safety habits to stay secure online. Let's create a comprehensive checklist that you can use every day and week to keep your digital life safe and organized.

## Daily Security Habits

Your daily digital safety routine should become as natural as putting on your seatbelt when you get in a car. Here's what your daily checklist might include:

## Morning Check

Your morning device security check is like ensuring your rooms and house are as you left them at night. You can do the following:

- Look for any strange account notifications
- Check if any apps need important security updates
- Make sure your device's antivirus is running properly
- Review for any strange friend requests or messages

## Before Bed Check:

Ensuring your device security is like checking on family members and then locking the doors at night to keep the house and everyone inside safe. Here are some steps you can take to enhance your device security:

- Log out of accounts on shared devices
- Check that important files are backed up
- Make sure your device's security features are enabled
- Review your social media privacy settings

## Weekly Security Tasks:

Consider weekly security tasks like your weekend chores, such as laundry or cleaning your room. The following weekly maintenance will help keep everything running smoothly:

- Review and delete unnecessary apps
- Clear your browser history and cookies

- Update passwords if needed
- Check privacy settings on all social media accounts
- Review app permissions on your devices
- Scan your devices for viruses or malware

## Family Discussion Guide

Photo: Adobe Photo Stock

Creating an open dialogue about digital safety with your family is crucial. Think of it like having a family meeting about household rules - everyone needs to be on the same page about what's safe and what's not. Here's how to have productive conversations about digital safety with your family.

### Starting the Conversation

Begin by sharing what you've learned about digital safety. You might say something like, "I learned some really interesting things about staying safe online, and I think it would be good if we could talk about our family's digital safety rules." Share specific examples of good digital habits you're trying to develop, and ask your family members about their concerns and experiences.

131

## Topics to Discuss with Your Family

Create a list of important topics to cover in your family discussions such as balancing screen time and offline activities, limits on sharing personal information and online connections, and strategies on handling difficult situations like cyberbullying or harassment. Remember to make these discussions regular - maybe once a month - to keep everyone updated and address new concerns as they arise.

## Emergency Contact List

Your digital emergency contact list is like having a list of emergency numbers by your phone - you hope you never need it, but it's crucial to have ready just in case. Let's create a comprehensive list of who to contact in different digital emergency situations.

## Creating Your Emergency Contacts

Organizing your emergency contacts by situation type is essential. Start with your immediate family contacts, which should include the work and cell numbers for your parent or guardian, your home phone number, and the contact information for other family members.

Next, be sure to include contacts for your school, such as your counselor and teachers, as they can be important during emergencies. Additionally, retain contact information for technical support from your device's manufacturer, especially in case your device is damaged, lost, or hacked.

It is also crucial to save the contacts for local police, a cyberbullying hotline, and online safety organizations. Keep this list in both digital format (stored securely) and in printed form in a safe location. Remember to update it regularly to ensure that all information remains current.

## Regular Security Audit Guide

Think of a security audit like a health check-up for your digital life - it's a thorough examination of all your online accounts, devices, and habits to make sure everything is working safely and securely. Let's create a guide for conducting regular security audits.

## Monthly Security Audit

Keeping up with the regular security updates is becoming critical, so it is significant to set aside time each month for a thorough security check:

**Account Review:**

- Check all account settings and privacy configurations
- Review connected apps and remove unnecessary ones
- Update security questions if needed
- Check for any suspicious activity

**Device Check:**

- Update all software and apps
- Review device storage and remove unnecessary files
- Check backup systems are working
- Test security features like Find My Device

## Quarterly Deep Dive

With the advent and usage of AI, cyber criminals have advanced their techniques and reach to damage device security. Therefore, conducting quarterly deep dives for maximum security is also important and can be ensured through:

**Password Updates:**

- Change important passwords
- Review and update password manager entries
- Check for any compromised passwords
- Update security questions and recovery options

**Digital Cleanup:**

- Review and organize important files
- Delete old accounts you no longer use
- Update emergency contact information
- Review and update security software

## Digital Safety Agreement Template

A digital safety agreement is like a contract between you and your family about how to use technology safely and responsibly. It helps everyone understand the rules and expectations for online behavior. Let's create a template that you can customize for your family's needs.

## Basic Agreement Structure

Your digital safety agreement should cover all important aspects of online safety:

---

**Device Usage:**

I agree to:

- o   Use devices in common family areas
- o   Follow agreed-upon time limits
- o   Ask permission before downloading new apps
- o   Keep devices away from water and protect them from damage


**Online Behavior:**

I will:

- o   Think before posting or sharing
- o   Only connect with people I know in real life
- o   Tell a trusted adult if something makes me uncomfortable
- o   Be kind and respectful in online interactions


**Privacy and Security:**

I promise to:

- o   Keep my passwords private
- o   Not share personal information online
- o   Ask before posting photos of others
- o   Use privacy settings on all accounts

---

## Customizing Your Agreement

Collaborate with your family to modify the agreement according to your needs by incorporating specific rules about:

- o   Screen time limits
- o   Appropriate apps and websites
- o   Social media usage
- o   Gaming guidelines
- o   Consequences for breaking rules
- o   Rewards for responsible behavior

Regularly review and update the digital safety agreement as you grow and technology evolves to protect yourself and your family from potential cyber threats.

## Conclusion

Your digital safety plan is like a shield that helps protect you while you explore and enjoy the online world. By following your personal security checklist, maintaining open family discussions, keeping emergency contacts ready, conducting regular security audits, and following your digital safety agreement, you're well-equipped to handle any digital challenges that come your way.

Remember, this plan isn't meant to restrict you - it's meant to give you the freedom to enjoy technology safely and confidently. Keep your plan updated as you grow and as technology changes, and don't be afraid to adjust it based on your experiences and needs.

### Moving Forward

Congratulations! You've completed your journey through this guide to digital safety. But remember, digital safety is an ongoing journey - technology keeps changing, and so do the ways we need to protect ourselves. Keep learning, stay alert, and help others learn about digital safety too. You're now equipped with the knowledge and tools to be a responsible and safe digital citizen. Use your powers wisely, and keep exploring the amazing possibilities of the digital world!

Now it's time to put everything you've learned into practice. Start with creating your personal security checklist, then work on implementing the other elements of your safety plan. Share what you've learned with friends and family, and help create a safer digital world for everyone. Good luck on your continued digital safety journey!

# Your Thought on Cyber Safety Plan

1. What are the most important elements of your personal security checklist?

```
```

2. How often do you review and update your safety measures? Set a schedule!

```
```

3. What topics would you include in a family discussion about digital safety?

```
```

# Did you know?

Your device has likely been part of a botnet at some point! Over 25% of all internet-connected devices have unknowingly been part of a botnet (a network of hijacked devices) used to attack other systems. Most owners never realize their device was involved!

# APPENDIX 1

## Glossary of Terms

**A - D**

Adware: Software that automatically shows advertisements on your device

Antivirus: Software that protects your device from viruses and malware

Authentication: The process of proving you are who you say you are online

Bandwidth: The amount of data that can be sent over an internet connection

Biometrics: Using body features (like fingerprints or face) to verify identity

Breach: When hackers break into a system or account

Cookies: Small files websites use to remember information about you

Cyberbullying: Using technology to harass, threaten, or embarrass someone

Digital Footprint: The trail of data you leave behind online

Doxxing: Sharing someone's private information online without permission

**E - H**

Encryption: Scrambling information so others can't read it without permission

Firewall: Software that helps block unauthorized access to your device

Geolocation: Technology that can identify where you are physically located

Hacking: Breaking into computer systems or accounts without permission

Hardware: The physical parts of computers and devices

HTTPS: Secure version of the protocol used to transfer data on the web

**I - L**

Identity Theft: Stealing someone's personal information to pretend to be them

IP Address: A unique number that identifies your device on the internet

Keylogger: Malicious software that records what you type

Link: A connection between web pages or files

Logout: To sign out of an account or system

**M - P**

Malware: Any software designed to harm your device or steal information

Password Manager: Software that securely stores your passwords

Phishing: Trying to trick people into sharing personal information

Popup: A window that appears automatically on your screen

Privacy Settings: Controls that let you decide who can see your information

**Q - T**

Ransomware: Malware that locks your files until you pay money

Router: Device that connects your home network to the internet

Spam: Unwanted emails or messages, often advertising

Spyware: Software that secretly watches what you do on your device

Trojan: Malware disguised as legitimate software

**U - Z**

Update: New software versions that fix problems or add features

URL: The address of a website

VPN: Virtual Private Network  helps keep your online activity private

Virus: Malicious software that can copy itself and infect devices

Worm: Malware that spreads itself through networks

# APPENDIX 2
## Safety Scenarios

### Scenario 1: The Strange Friend Request

You receive a friend request from someone claiming to be a student at your school. Their profile was created last week, they have only three posts, and while they say they know your best friend, you've never met them. However, they've sent you a friendly message saying they're new and want to make friends.

What would you do?

Option A: Accept the request since they seem nice

Option B: Message your best friend to verify if they know this person

Option C: Ignore the request and block the account

Option D: Report the account as suspicious

Discussion: Think about the risks and consequences of each option. What additional steps could you take to verify this person's identity?

### Scenario 2: The Game Trade Offer

While playing your favorite online game, another player offers you rare in-game items in exchange for your account details "just to transfer the items." They say it's completely safe and they've done this many times before.

What would you do?

Option A: Share your details to get the items

Option B: Ask them to trade normally through the game's system

Option C: Report them for suspicious behavior

Option D: Record the conversation and continue talking to gather evidence

Discussion: What are the potential risks? How could this be a scam?


## Scenario 3: The Viral Challenge

A new viral challenge is trending on social media. Many of your friends are participating, but it involves sharing personal information like your first pet's name, the street you grew up on, and your mother's maiden name.

What would you do?


Option A: Participate because everyone else is

Option B: Share fake information instead

Option C: Warn friends about security risks

Option D: Ignore the challenge

Discussion: Why might sharing this specific information be dangerous? What could scammers do with these details?

# APPENDIX 3

# Digital Safety Pledges

## Personal Digital Safety Pledge

I, [Your Name: _____ ], pledge to:

☐ Protect my personal information online

☐ Think before I post or share

☐ Use strong, unique passwords

☐ Keep my software updated

☐ Report suspicious activity

☐ Ask for help when needed

☐ Be kind and respectful online

☐ Stand up against cyberbullying

☐ Verify information before sharing

☐ Balance my online and offline life

[Sign: _____ and Date: _____ ]

# Family Online Safety Agreement

We, the [Family Name: _____ ] family, agree to:

☐ Communicate openly about online activities

☐ Support each other in maintaining digital safety

☐ Share concerns about online experiences

☐ Respect each other's digital privacy

☐ Help family members learn about online safety

☐ Create and follow family tech rules

☐ Have regular digital safety check-ins

☐ Keep emergency contact information updated

☐ Monitor and discuss screen time together

☐ Maintain a healthy balance with technology

[Family Members Sign:_____ and Date: _____ ]

## Digital Citizenship Commitment

As a digital citizen, I commit to:

☐ Contributing positively to online communities

☐ Respecting others' digital rights and privacy

☐ Creating and sharing responsibly

☐ Supporting others who need help online

☐ Learning continuously about digital safety

☐ Teaching others about online security

☐ Being honest in online interactions

☐ Protecting my digital reputation

☐ Using technology ethically

☐ Being an upstander against online harm

# APPENDIX 4
## Safety Challenges

### Challenge 1: 7-Day Digital Security Sprint
Complete one security task each day:

Day 1: Update all passwords

Day 2: Review privacy settings

Day 3: Clean up friend lists

Day 4: Update software

Day 5: Back up important files

Day 6: Remove unused apps

Day 7: Create emergency plans

### Challenge 2: Digital Detective Training
Practice these skills daily:

Spot fake news in your feed

Identify suspicious emails

Recognize scam messages

Verify information sources

Check image authenticity

Report security concerns

### Challenge 3: Online Safety Ambassador
Help others by:

Teaching a family member about security

Sharing safety tips with friends

Creating digital safety posters

Organizing a safety discussion

Reporting online dangers

Supporting cyberbullying victims

| Remember: | Complete these activities with adult supervision |
|---|---|
|  | Document your progress and lessons learned |
| | Share your experiences with others |
| | Update your knowledge regularly |
| | Stay alert for new digital safety challenges |
| | Celebrate your security achievements |

# APPENDIX 5

# Digital Security Master Checklists

## Daily Security Checklist

□ Check for important app/software updates

□ Review new friends/follow requests

□ Scan through notifications for suspicious activity

□ Log out of accounts on shared devices

□ Clear browser history and cookies if using public devices

□ Check that antivirus is running properly

□ Review any automatic social media tags

□ Verify recent account logins

□ Check for unauthorized app permissions

## Weekly Security Checklist

□ Run full device antivirus scan

□ Review app permissions

□ Clear browser cache and downloads

□ Check privacy settings on social media

□ Update passwords if needed

□ Review connected apps and remove unnecessary ones

□ Back up important files

□ Check for software updates

□ Review recent online purchases

□ Monitor gaming account activity

## Monthly Security Audit

☐ Change passwords for critical accounts

☐ Review and update emergency contacts

☐ Check for data breaches (haveibeenpwned.com)

☐ Update security questions

☐ Review linked devices and accounts

☐ Check backup systems

☐ Update privacy settings across all platforms

☐ Review third-party app access

☐ Test recovery methods

☐ Update security software

## Social Media Safety Checklist

☐ **Profile Privacy:**

- ☐ Set account to private

- ☐ Review who can see posts

- ☐ Control who can tag you

- ☐ Limit old post visibility

- ☐ Review blocked accounts

☐ **Content Safety:**

- ☐ Remove location data from photos

- ☐ Check image backgrounds for personal info

- ☐ Review tagged photos

- ☐ Audit friend/follower lists

- □ Remove sensitive personal information

□ **Connection Safety:**

- □ Verify friend requests

- □ Check message request settings

- □ Review group memberships

- □ Control who can message you

- □ Set comment restrictions

## Device Security Checklist

□ **Physical Security:**

- □ Set screen lock

- □ Enable remote wipe

- □ Encrypt device

- □ Install tracking software

- □ Secure SIM card

□ **App Security:**

- □ Update all apps

- □ Remove unused apps

- □ Check app permissions

- □ Disable unnecessary features

- □ Set app-specific passwords

□ **Network Security:**

- □ Enable firewall

- □ Use VPN when needed

- □ Secure Wi-Fi settings

- ☐ Disable auto-connect features

- ☐ Review bluetooth connections

## Gaming Account Security

☐ **Account Protection:**

- ☐ Use unique gaming passwords

- ☐ Enable two-factor authentication

- ☐ Set up recovery options

- ☐ Review linked accounts

- ☐ Check payment methods

☐ **In-Game Security:**

- ☐ Set privacy preferences

- ☐ Review friend lists

- ☐ Check trading settings

- ☐ Monitor recent activity

- ☐ Set spending limits

## Emergency Response Checklist

☐ **If Account Compromised:**

- ☐ Change password immediately

- ☐ Enable two-factor authentication

- ☐ Check for unauthorized changes

- ☐ Review connected apps

- ☐ Alert contacts if necessary

- ☐ Document suspicious activity

- □ Report to platform

**□ If Device Compromised:**

- □ Disconnect from internet

- □ Run security scan

- □ Back up important data

- □ Reset to factory settings

- □ Update all software

- □ Change all passwords

- □ Monitor accounts for suspicious activity

## Family Safety Checklist

**□ Communication:**

- □ Set family online rules

- □ Create device usage schedule

- □ Establish online boundaries

- □ Plan regular safety discussions

- □ Set up emergency procedures

**□ Monitoring:**

- □ Review privacy settings together

- □ Check browsing history

- □ Monitor app downloads

- □ Track screen time

- □ Review online friends/contacts

## New Device Setup Checklist

☐ **Initial Security:**

- ☐ Change default passwords

- ☐ Enable encryption

- ☐ Set up lock screen

- ☐ Install security software

- ☐ Configure automatic updates

☐ **Privacy Settings:**

- ☐ Review app permissions

- ☐ Set up user accounts

- ☐ Configure location services

- ☐ Set up backup system

- ☐ Enable find my device

## Digital Footprint Cleanup Checklist

☐ Regular Maintenance:

- ☐ Delete old accounts

- ☐ Remove outdated information

- ☐ Update privacy settings

- ☐ Clean up friend lists

- ☐ Review tagged content

- ☐ Delete unnecessary apps

- ☐ Clear old files and downloads

## Safe Browsing Checklist

☐ Browser Security:

- ☐ Use HTTPS everywhere

- ☐ Enable pop-up blocker

- ☐ Install security extensions

- ☐ Clear cookies regularly

- ☐ Update browser

- ☐ Review saved passwords

- ☐ Check for safe browsing features

| Remember: | Customize checklists based on your specific needs |
|---|---|
|  | Set calendar reminders for regular checks |
| | Keep printed copies in a safe place |
| | Update checklists as new security threats emerge |
| | Share relevant checklists with family members |
| | Document when each check was completed |
| | Note any issues found during checks |
| | Keep track of solutions implemented |

# APPENDIX 6
## Quick Reference Cards

**Emergency Response Card**

If Account Hacked:

1. Change password immediately
2. Enable 2FA
3. Check for unauthorized changes
4. Contact platform support
5. Alert trusted contacts
6. Monitor for suspicious activity
7. Document everything

**Password Safety Card**

Strong Password Rules:

1. Minimum 12 characters
2. Mix upper/lowercase
3. Include numbers/symbols
4. Avoid personal info
5. Unique for each account
6. Change every 3 months
7. Use a password manager

**Online Privacy Card**

Privacy Checklist:

1. Check privacy settings
2. Review friend lists
3. Monitor tagged content
4. Control app permissions
5. Limit location sharing
6. Manage public info
7. Regular privacy audits

# APPENDIX 6
## Parent's Guide

## Understanding Your Child's Digital World

In today's techsavvy environment, children are increasingly exposed to digital devices and online platforms from a young age. As parents and caregivers, it is crucial to navigate this digital landscape effectively to ensure our children's safety and wellbeing. Understanding the nuances of their digital world helps us foster healthy habits and mitigate potential risks. Here are some key areas to consider:

## Ageappropriate device access guidelines:

Establishing appropriate guidelines for when and how children should access devices is vital. Different age groups require different levels of supervision and types of content. Setting clear expectations can help children develop responsible habits.

## Screen time recommendations by age:

Understanding how much screen time is suitable for various age groups can aid in promoting a balanced lifestyle. Research shows that too much screen time can affect physical activity, sleep, and social interactions, so it's important to find a healthy balance.

## Popular apps and platforms overview:

Familiarity with the most commonly used apps and platforms among children helps parents stay informed about what their kids are engaging with online. Knowing the features, purposes, and potential risks of these platforms enables better conversations with children about their digital interactions.

## Common online risks and prevention:

The digital world presents risks such as cyberbullying, inappropriate content, and online predators. Learning about these dangers allows parents and caregivers to implement preventative measures and have constructive discussions with children about safe online behavior.

## Warning signs of digital issues:

Being aware of the warning signs that indicate a child may be struggling with digital issues, such as changes in behavior or mood, can help parents address problems early. Open communication and regular checkins can foster trust and encourage children to share their experiences.

By understanding these aspects of your child's digital world, you can create a supportive environment that promotes safe exploration while encouraging digital literacy and healthy habits.

## Conversation Starters

1. "What's your favorite thing to do online?"

2. "Have you seen anything online that made you uncomfortable?"

3. "What would you do if someone online asked for personal information?"

4. "How do you know if someone online is really who they say they are?"

5. "What do you think makes a strong password?"

## Family Tech Rules Template

☐ Device-free times and zones

☐ Content restrictions

☐ App download process

☐ Screen time limits

☐ Social media guidelines

☐ Gaming boundaries

☐ Online purchase rules

☐ Privacy requirements

☐ Safety check-ins

☐ Consequence system

## Family Safety Agreement Template

**Online Safety Rules:**

1. _____

2. _____

3. _____


Consequences:

1. _____

2. _____

3. _____


Parent Signature: _____

Child Signature: _____

Date: _____

# APPENDIX 7

# Glossary of Terms

## Useful Websites and Apps

- Common Sense Media (www.commonsensemedia.org)
- Internet Matters (www.internetmatters.org)
- Be Internet Awesome (beinternetawesome.withgoogle.com)

## Safety Tools and Software

**Free Options:**

- Microsoft Defender
- Avast Free Antivirus
- AVG AntiVirus Free

**Premium Plans:**

- Norton 360
- Bitdefender
- Kaspersky Security

## Password Managers

**Free Options:**

- Bitwarden
- LastPass (basic version)
- KeePass

**Family Plans:**

- 1Password Families
- LastPass Families
- Dashlane Family Plan

## Parental Control Tools

**Built-in Options:**

- Apple Screen Time
- Google Family Link
- Microsoft Family Safety

**Third-party Options:**

- Qustodio
- Norton Family
- Kaspersky Safe Kids

# Further Reading

## Books for Young Readers

"Staying Safe Online" by Louie Stowell

"Cybersecurity for Teens" by Peter H. Gregory

"The Smart Girl's Guide to Privacy" by Violet Blue

"Own Your Space: Keep Yourself and Your Stuff Safe Online" by Linda McCarthy

## Books for Parents

"Parenting in the Digital Age" by Bill Ratner

"Screenwise: Helping Kids Thrive in Their Digital World" by Devorah Heitner

"The Tech-Wise Family" by Andy Crouch

# ABOUT THE AUTHOR

Hafiz Afzaal is a passionate advocate for children's digital safety and well-being, driven by a deep concern about the growing challenges young people face in the digital world. Through extensive research and collaboration with cybersecurity experts, educators, and child safety professionals, they have compiled this comprehensive guide to help young people navigate the digital landscape safely.

Believing that every child deserves a safe and positive online experience, Hafiz has dedicated significant time to studying digital safety issues, consulting with experts, and gathering real stories from young people about their online experiences. Their motivation comes from witnessing how proper guidance and knowledge can empower children to make smart choices online and protect themselves from digital dangers.

Hafiz is particularly interested in making complex digital safety concepts accessible and engaging for young readers. He believes that understanding online safety shouldn't be intimidating or boring, but rather an empowering journey that helps children build confidence in their digital lives.

When not writing or researching about digital safety, he enjoys spending time with family, reading about emerging technologies, and exploring ways to make the digital world a better place for young people. He is a firm believer in the power of education and awareness in creating positive change in our increasingly connected world.